Bebe Black Carminito

The Curated Board

INSPIRED PLATTERS & SPREADS FOR ANY OCCASION

Foreword by Susan Spungen • *Photography by* Marie Reginato

CAMERON + COMPANY
Petaluma, California

CONTENTS

BREAKFAST & BRUNCH

MIDDAY GRAZING

FOREWORD

As the founding food editor of *Martha Stewart Living* magazine, I ran a test kitchen full of creative spirits. I got to mentor so many people, which was my favorite part of the job. I was lucky enough to do something I loved, and I wanted to help others find success in an industry that could be hard to break into. After my twelve years there, I went on to a freelance life as a food stylist for print and film, a cookbook author, and a recipe writer, but teaching has always been at the core of what I do.

I first met Bebe Black Carminito back in 2017 when she attended a baking workshop (specifically, apple pie baking) that I gave along with Yossy Arefi at my home in East Hampton. This was in the pre-pandemic era of Instagram-driven, live, in-person workshops. Workshops like these were popular not only as skill-building experiences but also as bonding experiences. Many of the women (yes, we were all women), made lasting friendships with the other participants, myself included.

When I taught an online class on recipe writing a few years later, Bebe was one of the first to sign up, and I was happy to see her familiar face among the students. Every time I had Bebe as a student, I was struck by her curiosity, her intensity, and her desire to learn and expand her culinary horizons.

As I followed Bebe's life through social media, I enjoyed seeing the artful boards that she and her husband, David, relished during the darkest days of the pandemic, when we were all cooking, cooking, cooking, and then cooking some more. It was such a lighthearted, easy, and fun way to make a meal out of all the bits and bobs in the house and to feel a little celebratory at the same time. Just seeing these delightful spreads put me in a good mood, while also reminding me that I could do the same—that every meal didn't need to be cooked and that, maybe, it could just be put together in a smart and beautiful way.

In the following years, Bebe has continued to devote herself to becoming a professional food stylist, recipe developer, and creator. With this book, she brings us her inspired take on the grazing trend, informed by her own experiences. Bebe's famously tiny and cheerful kitchen gives her and her recipes a sense of resourcefulness and economy born out of real life.

As we all know, and as Bebe proves here, good food can bring people together—no matter what your resources or circumstances are.

My particular background and specialty are in combining the delicious and the beautiful into one single gesture. I'm proud to have had a hand in mentoring and influencing Bebe and her work and to see her grow from a student into a teacher.

—Susan Spungen, cookbook author, food stylist, and recipe developer

INTRODUCTION

In the spring of 2020, during the early days of the pandemic, I started serving variations on charcuterie and cheese boards for my husband, David, and myself after long days of working at home. An array of foods for snacking and grazing seemed to be a perfect choice for casual dining during a time of chaos and uncertainty. This was also a way of slowing down, connecting, and celebrating "date night" as we jump-started the weekend. I would make a few things from scratch, trying out new recipes, while raiding my pantry, refrigerator, and freezer for the rest. My husband and I found delight in this weekly ritual, which happened nearly every Friday evening.

In 2017, before the pandemic began, I started an online monthly cookbook club called the #getcookingcookbookclub with my friend Steph Whitten. The club provided a platform for its members, a vibrant cookbook-loving community, to share their passion for cookbooks, home cooking, and recipes from around the world. Each month we choose female-authored works that are diverse in global cuisine. Being in this club allowed me to reach outside of my comfort zone to try new foods and ingredients. In a given week, I might make pizzetta, pot stickers, and/or pierogies from all different parts of the world.

My Instagram cookbook club inspired and informed the writing of this book and was the impetus for this project. Drawing inspiration from the club, I varied the ingredients of my boards, platters, spreads, and sheet pans, with an emphasis on making them visually beautiful and interesting as I incorporated varied aesthetic elements. And when the recipes needed testing for this book, members of my ardent cookbook family willingly offered to do so. Thanks to them, this book is a celebration of both food and community.

Throughout this journey, one thing I've learned is that you don't need a state-of-the-art kitchen with all the latest gadgets to create beautiful food. What you do need is a bit of imagination, a willingness to innovate and be flexible, and a vision. All of my recipes in this book were developed in the 70-square-foot kitchen of our 450-square-foot studio apartment. Before I moved in, David painted the kitchen a vibrant and bold orange—the color of Cara Cara oranges—and my kitchen is the happiest corner in my world.

This book is also meant to inspire you to create your own boards, platters, and spreads. There are infinite ways to combine and vary ingredients from a list of prepared foods like cheeses, jams, salsas, and crackers with your favorite homemade foods like dips, baked goods, and salads. Incorporate that tinned fish or spice medley you purchased on your travels. We invite you to explore your own heritage as well as others. Visit your local grocery stores for regional specialties, and your local farmers' markets for seasonal fruits, vegetables, and edible flowers.

Boards, platters, and spreads are super easy to put together with store-bought items from your pantry, and they can be made special with the addition of a homemade component or two. Each of the boards in this book is just a starting point, so feel free to mix and match to personalize, curate, and make yours exactly what you want it to be for any occasion.

As a food stylist and a professional makeup artist, I like to create beauty, so along the way, I'll give you plenty of easy tips that will take your creations over the top and make them works of art. I'll also give you plenty of advice on what to keep on hand in your pantry and fridge so you can whip up a board, platter, or spread at a moment's notice.

I hope you enjoy this quick and easy way to feed your family and entertain your guests. Here's to food, community, and everyday creativity.

"People who love to eat are always the best people."
—*Julia Child*

About This Book

The Curated Board includes twenty-eight boards, platters, and spreads, each with a different theme. There's one for every time of the day, from breakfast to lunch to snacking/grazing, dinner, and dessert. And each includes one or more recipes for homemade dishes to make your board special, as well as a list of store-bought accompaniments to fill out the selection of offerings. The recipes range from healthful to decadent, and all include a drinks suggestion for pairing, from cocktails to mocktails.

Each menu has a "Put It Together" section suggesting how to serve your board, platter, or sheet pan. Following many recipes, you will find baking, cooking, and recipe tips to make your home-cooked dishes their finest, along with variations to personalize your recipes. "Make It Beautiful" styling tips will help you garnish your work and decorate your boards, platters, or sheet pans to make them works of art. These simple and easy styling tips build on my experience as a food stylist for cookbooks, advertising and marketing, and social media posts.

There are seven special menus contributed by dear friends sprinkled throughout the book—all incredible cooks and leaders in the food industry. This collaboration was a perfect way to highlight my love of connecting with others through food. It has been an honor to work with them in this capacity and to share their beautiful recipes.

Tips for Creating Stylish Boards & Platters

PICK A THEME
First, choose a theme. It can be based on a color story; a special occasion such as a bridal shower, holiday, or birthday; or centered around a specific cuisine. The theme can also be geared toward the time of day, whether it's brunch, lunch, happy hour, or dessert.

KNOW YOUR GUESTS
Keep in mind how many people you are serving and who is on your guest list. All the menus and recipes in this book can easily be scaled up or down to accommodate a small gathering (like in my tiny house, where we can host a maximum of four guests) or a large party. Also, many of the recipes in this book are dietary friendly and can be made gluten-free, nut-free, dairy-free, vegan, or vegetarian depending on the store-bought items you choose and the recipes you make. Take note of any dietary restrictions and adjust as necessary.

ADD VISUAL INTEREST
Creating a board is also about creating a mood. Start by choosing a place to arrange your board and accompaniments on and add a dramatic, punchy, and/or colorful tablecloth or other surface. Choose bowls and other serveware to hold dips, condiments, nuts, and items that match the theme of the board or platter. Set out a stack of individual plates and an array of flatware for guests to use. These can be as styled as a vintage tea set for an English Tea Party (page 45) or an assortment of different styles and colors to create a unique look. Layer in color with napkins, and add drama with candles or flowers.

SELECT YOUR GLASSWARE
Choose glasses that are appropriate for the drinks you are serving. For example, flutes and coupes are ideal for bubbly and martini glasses are suitable for martinis. However, also feel free to get creative and use what you have on hand. An assortment of different glasses is also a nice touch. Be sure to have plenty of ice for drinks; use a colorful vintage ice bucket if you have one. Before setting out your glasses, use a glass-polishing cloth to remove any spots or residue.

CHOOSE SEASONALITY & ADD COLOR
When deciding what to serve, freshness, seasonality, and availability are the key factors that I rely on. I love adding colorful visual impact with edible flowers, verdant leaves, sprays of herbs, and microgreens. Remember, we feast with our eyes first so consider aesthetics, color, and beauty.

HAVE FUN!
The main goal of this book is to *have fun*. Not everything has to be homemade, in fact, I encourage you to only make one or two recipes and then shop your favorite bakeries, specialty food markets, cheese shops, florists, and farmers' markets to draw inspiration from to build your boards. As one of my favorite culinary icons Ina Garten says, "Store-bought is fine!" and honestly, nobody will know the difference. Being flexible and taking a shortcut here and there will give you more time for sharing precious moments—and having fun!—with your loved ones.

Pantry Staples

I like to keep an array of staples on hand for creating my menus at the last minute. Keeping basics like dried herbs, spices, condiments, vinegars, and a well-stocked bar means you always have ingredients at the ready. Also, snacks—olives, nuts, pickles—and jarred items, like marinated artichoke hearts, jams, salsa, and pesto, are the perfect finishing touches to any board.

SALT, PEPPER & OIL
For everyday use, I like kosher salt. Kosher salt differs between brands and I stick to Diamond Crystal. Flavored salts, like garlic salt, add a boost of zippy flavor, and flaky salt is a terrific finish. Grinding black peppercorns in a pepper mill will always give you the freshest flavor. I love pink peppercorns; lightly crush them instead of grinding for added flavor and color. For a milder oil that can tolerate high heat, I use avocado oil, and my go-to oil for vinaigrettes and finishing is always extra-virgin olive oil.

USING PEPPERS & CHILES
I use all types of peppers and chiles, from sweet bell peppers to Thai chiles. Wear gloves when touching spicy raw chiles, and be sure not to touch your eyes.

EDIBLE FLOWERS & FRESH HERBS
Edible flowers and fresh herbs add color and beauty to any board. Be sure that the flowers are unsprayed. The best sources are from your garden or local farmers' market. You can also find them online. These accompaniments will make your gatherings all the more convivial.

CHEESES & CHARCUTERIE
Keep a variety of cheeses on hand, like cow, goat, or sheep, with different textures and flavors, from fresh and creamy to aged and nutty. A good rule of thumb is to include three different cheeses, and the same rule applies to charcuterie. A selection of cured salami, prosciutto, and mortadella would be ideal on any board. For any recipes that call for shredded cheese, be sure to use freshly shredded for the best results.

FRESH FRUIT & VEGETABLES
Always buy the freshest fruit and vegetables you can find, ideally in season. And whenever possible, I make it a point to support local farmers' markets and other local grocers.

Tools for Making Things Beautiful

This is an abbreviated list, but it contains my most-used items when I'm food styling, and is a great starting point to help make your boards, trays, sheet pans, and platters visually appealing. You may already have some of these in your kitchen.

PASTRY BRUSHES & PAINT BRUSHES
Use clean pastry brushes for adding egg wash or brushing on oil. Use paint brushes to brush away crumbs or add oil or water to make things glisten

FOAM COSMETIC WEDGES
Great for wiping away a spill or unwanted elements

FUNNELS
Use these to transfer liquids into other containers without spilling

GEL FOOD COLORING
Adds color to an array of foods

GLASS-POLISHING CLOTHS
Removes unsightly water spots

KITCHEN BOUQUET
Great for browning foods and adding color

KITCHEN BLOWTORCH
Used to brûlée or add a bit of char

KNIVES
An array of types and sizes; be sure they are sharpened

OFFSET SPATULAS
Large and small sizes are excellent for transferring food, smoothing a surface, and spreading

PASTRY BAGS & TIPS
Choose reusable silicone bags and a set of round and star tips for piping neatly

Q-TIPS
Excellent for removing drops of liquid or to blot away a small spill

RULER
Great for ensuring even measures

SCISSORS
In various sizes, for snipping herbs and more

SILICONE SPATULAS
Good for smoothing out surfaces, scraping dips into bowls, and more

SKEWERS
Both wooden and bamboo skewers, in an array of sizes, are great for spearing small bites, veggies, fruits, and more

SPOONS, SMALL & TINY
Perfect for sauces and condiments

SPRAY BOTTLE, SMALL
To spritz and refresh fruits and veggies

SQUEEZE BOTTLES
Excellent for drizzling sauces or olive oil

TOOTHPICKS
Regular toothpicks help with spearing things in place and party picks are excellent for serving small finger foods

TWEEZERS
For placing small flowers and herbs, or removing unwanted items

BREAKFAST & BRUNCH

From light to luxurious, this chapter showcases boards, platters, spreads, plates, and sheet pans heaped with seasonal fruits, granola, bagels, smoked salmon, chopped salads, falafel, pita breads, waffles, and fruit compotes. Perfect for families and weekend guests, some boards can be left out for grazing, while hot foods such as waffles and toasted bagels will tempt early risers. Indulge in our cocktail recipes, alcoholic or not, for weekend brunches.

WAFFLES, BERRIES & BUBBLES, OH MY!

This weekend brunch board features lofty Belgian waffles with a wide variety of toppings. Raspberry mimosas are the perfect complement. The waffle batter works in both Belgian and standard waffle irons; cooking times may vary.
Serves 4 to 6

Cinnamon–Oat Belgian Waffles (page 18)
Berry–Vanilla Compote (page 19)
Raspberry Mimosas (page 19)

ACCOMPANIMENTS
Nut butter, such as peanut, almond, or cashew
Pure Grade-A maple syrup and/or berry syrup
Salted European-style butter
Fresh raspberries, strawberries, and/or blueberries
Confectioners' sugar, for dusting waffles

TO DRINK
Coffee, tea, and/or Raspberry Mimosas

PUTTING IT TOGETHER
You will need a medium wooden board, platter, or big plate for the waffles. You will also need a few small bowls and spoons for the toppings, plus a small fine-mesh sieve or shaker for dusting the waffles with confectioners' sugar.

Cinnamon–Oat Belgian Waffles

Oat flour and oat milk lend a nutty flavor to these showy waffles with deep pockets for catching flavorful toppings. They are terrific topped with mixed berry compote, berry syrup, and/or fresh berries. If you like, dust these with confectioners' sugar for an elegant finish.

Makes 4 waffles

1½ cups (190 g) plus 2 tablespoons all-purpose flour

½ cup (45 g) plus 2 tablespoons oat flour

½ cup (65 g) cornstarch

¼ cup (50 g) sugar

1 teaspoon baking powder

½ teaspoon baking soda

1 tablespoon ground cinnamon

1 tablespoon kosher salt

2 cups (480 ml) oat milk

⅔ cup (165 ml) canola oil

2 teaspoons vanilla extract

2 large eggs, lightly beaten

Toppings

Berry–Vanilla Compote (opposite)

Butter, maple syrup, and/or nut butters

Fresh fruit

Preheat the oven to 250°F (120°C).

In a large bowl, whisk together the all-purpose flour, oat flour, cornstarch, sugar, baking powder, baking soda, cinnamon, and salt. In a medium bowl, whisk together the oat milk, oil, vanilla, and eggs until thoroughly combined.

Make a well in the center of the dry ingredients and add the liquids. Whisk together just until blended; don't overmix. Set the batter aside to rest for 20 to 30 minutes at room temperature. You will see small bubbles forming on the batter during this phase. The batter will be thick.

Heat a Belgian waffle iron and spray it lightly with cooking spray. Using a measuring cup, add batter to the prepared waffle iron, close the lid, and cook until golden brown or done to your liking, 4½ to 5 minutes or according to the manufacturer's directions. Transfer the waffle to a sheet pan and place in the oven to keep warm. Repeat to make 4 waffles. Serve hot, with the toppings of your choice.

COOKING TIP
To make these ahead, let cool, place in a zippered plastic freezer bag, and freeze for up to 2 months. Reheat in a toaster oven.

Vegan Belgian Waffles: Make 2 flax eggs by combining ⅓ cup (45 g) ground flaxseed and ½ cup (120 ml) boiling water in a small bowl. Let stand for 5 to 7 minutes, stirring occasionally. Replace the eggs in the main recipe with the mixture. The batter will have a much thicker consistency and the bubbles on the surface won't be as visible.

MAKE IT BEAUTIFUL If you dust the waffles with confectioners' sugar when they are still warm, the sugar will dissipate quickly. Let them cool down just a tad for snowy visibility. Serve these waffles with a small dish of butter balls alongside. Place a stick of cold butter in the freezer for 10 to 12 minutes, then use a melon baller to scoop it into balls.

Berry-Vanilla Compote

Serve this sweet-tart compote with Cocoa-Coconut-Maple Granola (page 22), whip it into a smoothie, or use it as a dessert sauce. This recipe reminds me of late-night visits to Marie Callender's eating their "razzleberry" pie à la mode with my mom. Strawberries and/or blueberries can also be used in this recipe.

Makes about 2½ cups (600 ml)

1 heaping cup (6 ounces/170 g) blackberries, halved if large

1 heaping cup (6 ounces/170 g) raspberries

3 tablespoons sugar

1 teaspoon vanilla extract

In a small saucepan over low heat, combine the berries, sugar, and vanilla extract. Simmer, stirring often, until thickened, about 20 minutes, crushing a few of the berries with the back of a wooden spoon halfway through cooking. Remove from the heat and let cool completely. Refrigerate in a glass jar with a tight-fitting lid for up to 1 week.

MAKE IT BEAUTIFUL Reserve a handful of fresh berries to adorn the compote-topped waffles, and add a few fresh berries to the compote bowl to give it some visual contrast.

Raspberry Mimosas

A sweet take on the classic cocktail using homemade raspberry syrup. These are so easy to make, and the color is beautiful!

Makes 4 drinks

Raspberry Syrup

¾ cup (180 ml) water

¾ cup (150 g) sugar

1 heaping cup (6 ounces/170 g) fresh or frozen raspberries

2 tablespoons fresh lemon juice

¼ cup (60 ml) fresh orange juice

Prosecco or Champagne, well chilled

Fresh raspberries, for garnish (optional)

Fresh mint sprigs or leaves, for garnish (optional)

To make the syrup, in a saucepan, combine the water and sugar. Simmer over medium heat until the sugar is dissolved. Add the raspberries and lemon juice. Reduce the heat to low and simmer until syrupy, 25 to 30 minutes, pressing the raspberries with a small spatula to release their juices about halfway through. Remove from the heat and let cool to room temperature, about 30 minutes. Strain the syrup twice through a fine-mesh sieve set over a bowl to remove seeds and berry pulp. Discard the solids and transfer the syrup to a jar with a tight-fitting lid. Refrigerate for at least 2 hours or up to 1 week.

To make the mimosas, add 1 tablespoon orange juice to each of four Champagne flutes. Stir 2 tablespoons of the raspberry syrup into each flute, then top each off with the bubbly of your choosing. Garnish each with a few fresh raspberries and/or mint, if desired. Serve immediately.

GRANOLA, FRUIT & YOGURT BOARD

This board is a light and healthy way to start your day. Here, homemade Cocoa-Coconut Maple Granola is accompanied by Berry-Vanilla Compote, plenty of seasonal fresh fruit, yogurt or milk, and lots of extra toppings.
Serves 4 to 6

Cocoa–Coconut–Maple Granola (page 22)
Berry–Vanilla Compote (page 19)

ACCOMPANIMENTS
Nut butters, coconut flakes, and honey
Fresh seasonal fruit, such as sliced peaches, mixed berries, or orange slices
Yogurt and/or milk

TO DRINK
Coffee or green tea

PUTTING IT TOGETHER
Serve all the elements of this recipe on a medium wooden cutting board, platter, or tray. You will need a medium bowl for the granola and another for the fresh fruit, as well as several small bowls for the berry compote, yogurt, nut butter, coconut, and honey. Add spoons and individual bowls for the granola, small spoons for the toppings, a little pitcher for the milk, and a honey dipper. For decorating, we took advantage of blood orange and kumquat season, but feel free to decorate with any seasonal fruits.

Cocoa–Coconut–Maple Granola

This recipe marries granola and chocolate, two of my favorite foods, with other best-loved ingredients like coconut flakes, pecans, cinnamon, and maple syrup. The granola isn't too sweet, so feel free to top it with Berry-Vanilla Compote (page 19), your favorite nut butter, yogurt, fresh fruit, and/or extra flakes of toasted coconut. If you like, swap out the pecans for other nuts, such as almonds, walnuts, or cashews.

Makes 4½ cups (1 L) | Serves 4 to 6

- 2¼ cups (200 g) old-fashioned oats (not instant or quick-cook)
- ¾ cup (35 g) unsweetened coconut chips
- ½ cup (50 g) raw pecans, coarsely chopped or halved
- ¼ cup (25 g) unsweetened cocoa powder, Dutch processed
- ½ teaspoon kosher salt
- ½ teaspoon ground cinnamon
- ¼ cup (55 g) plus 2 tablespoons packed light brown sugar
- ¼ cup plus 1 tablespoon (75 ml) coconut oil, melted
- ¼ cup plus 1 tablespoon (75 ml) pure Grade-A maple syrup
- ½ teaspoon vanilla extract

Line a sheet pan with parchment paper. Arrange an oven rack in the center of the oven and preheat the oven to 325°F (165°C).

In a large bowl, combine the oats, coconut, pecans, cocoa powder, salt, and cinnamon and stir to mix. In a small bowl, combine the brown sugar with the melted coconut oil, maple syrup, and vanilla and stir to blend. Pour the coconut oil mixture over the oats and stir with a rubber spatula, being sure to coat the oats thoroughly. Spread onto the prepared sheet pan in an even layer and bake until slightly crispy, 20 to 25 minutes, flipping with a spatula every 10 minutes and rotating the pan for even baking. Remove from the oven and let cool on a wire rack for about 20 minutes; the granola will crisp up as it cools. Store in an airtight container at room temperature for about 1 week.

BAKING TIP

Most granolas are done when they turn a light brown, but this one is coated in cocoa powder, so you can't judge its doneness by the color. When the oats start to look a little matte when you flip and toss them, you will notice a crispier texture. The coconut and nuts will also appear lightly toasted when the granola is done, and a chocolate aroma will permeate the kitchen.

MAKE IT BEAUTIFUL Add vibrant color to this board by decorating it with seasonal fruit. Because of the addition of cocoa powder, the coconut and pecans become dark when baked. To highlight them as a garnish, toast a handful of each on the side (without the cocoa): Using two separate small sheet pans, toast the coconut in the preheated oven until lightly golden, 4 to 5 minutes. Toast the pecans for 8 minutes. Use to garnish the granola.

PESCATARIAN CHALLAH BAGEL BRUNCH

This gorgeous challah bagel brunch board is from dietitian, photographer, and author Micah Siva. Her love for cooking started in her grandmother's kitchen, which paved the way to her career, where she shares her love for Jewish cuisine with a twist. This menu showcases smoked salmon or lox along with hummus and all the fixings. **Serves 4 to 6**

Everything Challah Bagels (page 26)
Everything Bagel Seasoning (page 28)
Everything Bagel–Seasoned Hummus (page 29)
Quick–Pickled Shallots (page 81)

ACCOMPANIMENTS
Smoked salmon or lox
Cream cheese and/or herbed chèvre
Fresh dill and chives
Lemon wedges
Sliced tomatoes and cucumbers
Baby rainbow carrots and radishes
Dill pickles and capers
Edible flowers, such as fennel and chive blossoms

TO DRINK
Coffee, tea, and/or Raspberry Mimosas (page 19)

PUTTING IT TOGETHER
Use a large wooden board, platter, or tray. Add small bowls for the Quick–Pickled Shallots, dill pickles, capers, and Everything Bagel Seasoning, and ramekins for the cream cheese and Everything Bagel–Seasoned Hummus. Place the chèvre on a small plate with extra herbs on the board and accompanying cheese spreaders alongside the salmon or lox slices, dill sprigs, and slices of lemon, tomatoes, and cucumbers. We also added more punch with rainbow carrots, radishes, and extra chives on the board. Have small plates nearby for guests to build their own challah bagel brunch. The bagels can also be toasted right before assembly.

Everything Challah Bagels

In this fun spin on a classic bagel, challah dough is twisted into a bagel shape and topped with Everything Bagel Seasoning just before baking. Serve the bagels fresh and hot out of the oven or split and toasted with butter, hummus, cream cheese, or fresh chèvre. These challah bagels have a lighter and fluffier texture than a classic chewy, dense bagel.

Makes 12 bagels

1 package (2¼ teaspoons) active dry yeast

1 tablespoon sugar

1 cup (240 ml) warm (110°F/43°C) water

2 large eggs, at room temperature, lightly whisked

⅓ cup (75 ml) olive oil

¼ cup (60 ml) honey

1 teaspoon kosher salt

4½ cups (565 g) all-purpose flour

1 large egg beaten with 1 teaspoon water, for egg wash

¼ cup (30 g) Everything Bagel Seasoning (page 28)

Line two sheet pans with parchment paper and coat a large bowl with olive oil.

In the bowl of a stand mixer, combine the yeast, sugar, and ½ cup (120 ml) of the water. Stir to blend. Let stand until foamy, 5 to 10 minutes. Add the remaining ½ cup (120 ml) water, the eggs, oil, honey, and salt. Using the paddle attachment, beat on low speed until blended, 1 to 2 minutes.

Switch to the dough hook and add the flour 1 cup (125 g) at a time, mixing on low speed. Increase the speed to medium and knead until the dough is smooth and not sticky, 5 to 7 minutes.

Transfer the dough to the prepared bowl (use a bowl scraper to remove it from the mixer) and place it in a warm area that is draft-free. Cover the bowl with a clean damp towel. Let rise until doubled in size, 1 to 2 hours.

Punch down the dough to remove any air bubbles and transfer it to a lightly floured surface. Divide the dough into 12 pieces. Shape each piece into a rope about 15 inches (38 cm) long, spacing six on each of the prepared sheet pans. Cover each with a damp towel and let rise for 15 minutes.

Arrange two oven racks in the lower half of the oven and preheat the oven to 350°F (175°C).

Cut each rope in half and twist both pieces into a circle, tucking in the end to close and pinching to seal. Return to the sheet pans, cover again with damp towels, and let rise for 20 minutes.

Using a pastry brush, brush the tops of the bagels evenly with the egg wash and sprinkle the seasoning evenly over each one. Bake both sheet pans in the oven until golden brown, 20 to 25 minutes, rotating the pans halfway through baking. Let cool for 5 minutes on the pans on a wire rack, then place the bagels

continued...

continued...

directly on the racks. These can be served while still warm or at room temperature. To toast, use a sharp serrated knife and cut the bagels in half. The bagels are best eaten the day they are made. Freeze the remaining bagels in an airtight container for up to 2 months.

BAKING TIP

The length of time for proofing dough always depends on the temperature of the room where it is rising. The dough is done proofing when doubled in size and when pressed gently with a fingertip, it barely springs back and doesn't collapse.

MAKE IT BEAUTIFUL Everything Bagel Seasoning adds texture and crunch to these bagels. Brush the egg wash on the bagels evenly for uniform golden color and sprinkle on the spice mix evenly as well. Use the homemade Everything Bagel Seasoning, or feel free to use your favorite store-bought blend. Have a few extra crushed pink peppercorns on hand to garnish the bagels if they get too dark in the oven.

Everything Bagel Seasoning

This may not have *everything* in it, but it has seeds, herbs, spices, and salt.
Feel free to add your own favorites or omit one or more of these ingredients.

Makes ⅓ cup (45 g)

1 tablespoon sesame seeds, toasted (see Cooking Tip)

1 tablespoon black sesame seeds

1 tablespoon fennel seeds

1 tablespoon poppy seeds

1 tablespoon dried minced onion

1 teaspoon dill seeds

1 teaspoon flaky salt

½ teaspoon pink peppercorns, crushed with a mortar and pestle

¼ teaspoon garlic salt

In a small bowl, mix all the ingredients together. Store in a small, airtight jar for up to 6 months.

COOKING TIP

Toasting sesame seeds: Preheat the oven to 350°F (175°C). Spread ½ cup (60 g) white sesame seeds on a small rimmed sheet pan and toast, shaking the pan halfway through, until lightly golden, about 8 minutes. Be sure to keep your eye on them as they can quickly burn. Let cool completely on the sheet pan set on a wire rack. Transfer to a jar with a tight-fitting lid and store in your pantry.

Everything Bagel–Seasoned Hummus

This hummus recipe is so easy that you will never buy hummus from the store again. It comes together in a flash, quicker than you can say "Everything Bagel Seasoning," which is the ingredient that takes it to another level. Using the chickpea liquid from the can lends to the velvety, silky texture of this hummus.

Makes about 1½ cups (360 ml)
Serves 6 to 8

One 15-ounce (430-g) can low-sodium chickpeas

¼ cup (60 g) tahini, stirred well

3 tablespoons Everything Bagel Seasoning (opposite)

¼ teaspoon grated lemon zest

2 tablespoons fresh lemon juice (about 1 small lemon)

2 cloves garlic

¼ cup (60 ml) extra-virgin olive oil, plus more for drizzling

Ground sumac, for garnish (optional)

Drain the chickpeas, reserving ¼ cup (60 ml) of the liquid. Transfer the chickpeas to a blender or food processor. Add the tahini, 2 tablespoons of the bagel seasoning, the lemon zest and juice, and garlic.

Puree the mixture on low speed, drizzling in the ¼ cup (60 ml) olive oil and the reserved chickpea liquid until smooth. Serve in a bowl, drizzled with olive oil and sprinkled with the remaining 1 tablespoon bagel seasoning and the sumac, if using.

Serve immediately, or refrigerate in an airtight container for up to 4 days.

VARIATION
For a plain hummus, omit the Everything Bagel Seasoning and season to taste.

MAKE IT BEAUTIFUL Reserve a few whole chickpeas to garnish the hummus. Add a little bowl of extra spice mix to the board for guests who want to sprinkle more over their hummus. I also like to add a few crushed pink peppercorns to the tops of the hummus and bagels for extra color.

LEBANESE SHEET PAN BRUNCH

This brunch menu stars some of my favorite Lebanese dishes: falafel, tabbouleh, and pita breads. A selection of dips, crunchy and pickled vegetables, and fresh herbs add color and flavor to these standout brunch foods. Katia Berberi and Steve Drapeau, owners of Bay Area food business, Anne's Toum, provided their family tabbouleh recipe, jars of their toum, and the overall inspiration for this menu. **Serves 4 to 6**

Crispy Baked Falafel (page 32)
Tabbouleh (page 33)
Hummus (page 29, see variation)

ACCOMPANIMENTS

Baba ghanoush, tahini, and toum (Lebanese garlic sauce)

Herb-marinated feta

Olive oil mixed with za'atar

Torn pita breads, warmed

Sliced tomatoes, red onions, and red radishes

Cucumber spears

Baby arugula

Grapes

Olives, marinated artichokes, and Lebanese pickles

Fresh herbs such as dill, parsley, and/or mint

Pomegranate arils, for garnishing

TO DRINK

Arak (anise-flavored Lebanese liquor) or mint lemonade, served cold in chilled glasses

PUTTING IT TOGETHER

Line a small sheet pan with parchment paper. Arrange the falafel, sliced red onions, cucumber spears, torn pita, and herbs on the sheet pan. Put the sliced tomatoes and grapes on a small plate. Use bowls for the Tabbouleh, Hummus, baba ghanoush, tahini, toum, and radishes, as well as the olive oil, olives, artichokes, and Lebanese pickles; accompany with serving spoons. Allow your guests to fill the pitas with the falafel, arugula, herbs, and feta and, if desired, dip in the olive oil. Garnish the offerings with herb sprigs and pomegranate arils.

Crispy Baked Falafel

Baked falafel—patties of ground chickpeas—are healthy, herbaceous, and versatile. Tuck them into pita bread along with hummus, tahini, tabbouleh, and fresh veggies, or serve the falafel on top of a salad with feta. Here, it's shaped into patties and baked until golden and crispy.

Makes 16 falafel | Serves 4

1½ tablespoons avocado oil

One 15-ounce (430-g) can chickpeas, drained, rinsed, and patted dry with paper towels

1 cup (50 g) coarsely chopped fresh flat-leaf parsley

¾ cup (95 g) diced white onion

3 cloves garlic, peeled

1 teaspoon ground coriander

1 teaspoon ground cumin

1 teaspoon cayenne pepper

1 teaspoon garlic salt

Grated zest of 1 lemon

¼ teaspoon red pepper flakes (optional)

3 tablespoons white sesame seeds, toasted (see page 28)

2 tablespoons all-purpose flour

Preheat the oven to 375°F (190°C). Evenly coat a large rimmed sheet pan with the avocado oil and set aside.

In the bowl of a food processor, pulse the chickpeas, parsley, onion, garlic, spices, garlic salt, lemon zest, and red pepper flakes, if using, to create a fine meal that will hold together. Test by forming a tablespoonful into a ball. If it doesn't hold together, pulse the mixture a few more times.

Spoon the mixture into a bowl and add the sesame seeds and flour. Mix together with your hands just until no traces of flour appear; don't overwork the mixture.

Using a small ice-cream scoop or a tablespoon, form the mixture into 1½-inch (4-cm) balls and place on the prepared sheet pan about 1 inch (2.5 cm) apart. Press the balls into thick patties. Cover and refrigerate for at least 1 hour or for up to overnight.

Bake, gently turning them halfway through, until golden brown, 22 to 24 minutes. Let cool on the sheet pan for 5 minutes, then, using a metal spatula, transfer them to a wire rack. Serve warm or at room temperature.

COOKING TIP
To reheat the falafel, place them on a small sheet pan and place in a preheated 350°F (175°C) oven for 7 to 8 minutes, turning halfway through.

MAKE IT BEAUTIFUL Brush warm falafel with a little olive oil and plate them with fresh herb sprigs.

Tabbouleh

This herbed–bulgur salad is a perfect dish for brunch, lunch, picnics, and grazing at any time of day. It can be made one day in advance, adding the tomatoes right before serving.

Serves 4

1 cup (35 g) finely chopped curly parsley

1 cup (180 g) finely chopped tomatoes

¼ cup (10 g) finely chopped fresh mint

¼ cup (35 g) finely diced onion

⅛ to ¼ cup (18 to 35 g) fine bulgur wheat, cooked according to package directions and cooled

¼ cup (60 ml) fresh lemon juice

¼ cup (60 ml) olive oil

Kosher salt

In a medium bowl, combine the parsley, tomatoes, mint, and onion. Add the cooked bulgur. In a small bowl, whisk together the lemon juice and olive oil and toss with the salad to coat. Season with salt. Serve at once. Leftovers can be stored in an airtight container in the refrigerator for up to 2 days.

MAKE IT BEAUTIFUL Decorate the bowl of tabbouleh with sprigs of fresh mint and parsley.

FILIPINO MERIENDA BOARD

Merienda is a light meal or a selection of sweet or savory snacks served before a main meal. Originating in Spain and found today throughout regions of the world previously colonized by Spain, it was adopted by Filipinos and is served with an array of Filipino accompaniments. The cheese spread is from Rezel Kealoha, a Filipino food photographer and stylist, and is based on her grandmother's recipe. **Serves 4**

Pimento Cheese Spread (page 37)

ACCOMPANIMENTS
Pandesal (a Filipino bread roll, typically eaten for breakfast)
Saltine crackers, preferably SkyFlakes brand (Filipino crackers)
On-the-vine grape tomatoes
Cornichons, atchara (pickled green papaya)
Microgreens, edible flowers

TO DRINK
Iced ginger tea

PUTTING IT TOGETHER
Place a bowl of the Pimento Cheese Spread in the center of a medium wooden board, with a small serving paddle or knife alongside. Add the cornichons and atchara to small bowls and arrange around the cheese spread, along with the tomatoes. Decorate the board with edible flowers and microgreens, such as fennel blossoms and a microgreen medley. Place the crackers and pandesal on small plates alongside.

Pimento Cheese Spread

Colorful and packed with flavor, this Filipino and vegan version of the Southern favorite is made with vegan Cheddar, cream cheese, and mayonnaise, which can be found at most well-stocked supermarkets. Rather than using store-bought jarred peppers like most pimento cheese recipes, Rezel's family recipe makes use of freshly roasted red bell peppers.

Makes 1½ cups (360 ml) | Serves 4

1 red bell pepper

Olive oil, for brushing

2 cups (230 g) shredded vegan Cheddar cheese

2 tablespoons vegan cream cheese, at room temperature

1 tablespoon vegan mayonnaise

Salt and freshly ground black pepper

Preheat the oven or a toaster oven to 300°F (150°C).

Core, seed, and cut the pepper into quarters. Place on a small sheet pan, skin side up, and brush with olive oil. Bake until softened, about 30 minutes, turning them halfway through.

Wrap the pepper quarters in aluminum foil and let cool to room temperature, about 30 minutes. Unwrap the foil and peel off the skin of the pepper. Cut the quarters into thin strips and then dice them into small squares.

Place the shredded cheese in a food processor and pulse three to five times just to make the cheese shreds smaller; don't overdo it. Add the cream cheese and the mayonnaise. Pulse again two to five times to mix and bind the cheese together. Add the diced red pepper and pulse once to mix. Season to taste with salt and pepper.

Using a narrow rubber spatula, transfer the spread to a bowl. Serve at once or cover and refrigerate for at least 1 hour or up to overnight. Let sit at room temperature for 15 minutes before serving.

MAKE IT BEAUTIFUL Don't overmix the spread; it should remain chunky, with visible pieces of pepper. Garnish the top of the spread with a few reserved squares of pepper, if you like.

MIDDAY GRAZING

G razing boards are perfect for lazy weekends, especially if you have children and/or weekend guests. The boards in this chapter showcase cuisines from around the world, from an English tea party to a Ukrainian celebration to nachos from the American Southwest. Tinned fish and Tater Tots star on a board alongside another dedicated to Julia Child. And the picnic board is meant to be served al fresco, either in your backyard or in a park near you.

TATERS, TINNED FISH & TONICS

Conserved fish in colorful tins—called conservas in Spain and Portugal—are friends to food boards, platters, and trays. This board was inspired by my friend Maddie, who pairs her canned seafood with tonic-based cocktails to complement the rich flavors of the fish. Potatoes are a heavenly match for tinned fish, whether in the form of salty potato chips or Tater Tot "boats" topped with dollops of crème fraîche and a sprinkle of fresh dill. **Serves 4 to 6**

Tater Tot Boats (page 42)
Italian Gin & Tonics (page 43)

ACCOMPANIMENTS

Two or three kinds of tinned fish, such as smoked trout, marinated mackerel, and spicy salmon

Jammy boiled eggs with minced chives

Crostini (page 108)

Endive leaves and Persian cucumber spears

Small bunches of grapes

Lemon wedges

Fresh dill sprigs

Potato chips and/or crunchy spicy quicos (giant, crunchy corn kernels)

Olives and salted capers

Crème fraîche or sour cream, toum (Lebanese garlic sauce), Sriracha aioli, and/or chili crisp

TO DRINK
Italian Gin & Tonics

PUTTING IT TOGETHER

Place the Tater Tot boats on a large platter. Leave the tinned fish in their tins, with the covers opened and several fish forks for easy serving, and set alongside the platter. Arrange the crostini, cucumber spears, grapes, and lemon wedges on the platter. Garnish with the dill sprigs. Place the endive spears and jammy eggs on small individual plates. Place the potato chips and quicos in medium bowls. Serve the olives, capers, and sauces in small bowls with small serving spoons.

Tater Tot Boats

Whether served as a side dish or transformed into waffles, casseroles, or "totchos," (a version of nachos), Tater Tots are many people's childhood favorite. Here, they're baked into little "boats" to carry a cargo of tinned fish, herbs, and crème fraîche or sour cream. You'll only need a portion of a bag of frozen mini Tater Tots for this recipe, so save the rest for making more of these another time, or just for a late-night snack.

Makes 12 mini boats | Serves 4

Avocado or canola oil, for brushing

48 mini Tater Tots (about 222 g)
(see Cooking Tips)

~<<<

Toppings

Tinned fish, such as smoked trout, marinated mackerel, and spicy salmon

Crème fraîche or sour cream

Toum (Lebanese garlic sauce), preferably Anne's Toum

Sriracha aioli and/or chili crisp

Capers

Fresh dill

Preheat the oven to 425°F (220°C). Lightly brush each cup of a 12-cup nonstick mini muffin pan with the oil.

In each muffin cup, add 4 mini Tater Tots, placing two lengthwise and then two crosswise on top in each cup. Bake for 10 minutes, then remove the pan from the oven. Using a pestle, small jar, or a shot glass, press down gently but firmly in each cup to form the Tater Tots into small bowl-shaped vessels.

Bake again until very golden and crispy, 13 to 16 minutes. Using an offset spatula, transfer them to a wire rack to cool slightly. Serve the toppings alongside for diners to fill, or fill the Tater Tot "boats" with the tinned fish and toppings. Serve at once.

COOKING TIPS

If you can't find mini Tater Tots, use 24 regular-sized ones, adding two to each muffin cup. For a different take, fill these boats with your favorite toppings, such as sour cream, bacon, and chives. Or try my friend Katie's version: honey mustard, aioli, and fried capers.

Italian Gin & Tonics

Aperitivo Cappelletti, an Italian red bitters and wine-based aperitif, has a sweet, herbal flavor. Combined with gin, and sweet vermouth, it gives a gin and tonic an Italian twist that's both refreshing and complex. If you can't find Cappelletti, substitute with Aperol or Campari. A sprig of fresh rosemary and a bit of lemon juice complete this cocktail. Cin cin!

Makes 1 drink

1 fl. ounce (30 ml) gin, preferably Malfy Gin

½ fl. ounce (15 ml) sweet vermouth

½ fl. ounce (15 ml) Aperitivo Cappelletti

Tonic water, seltzer, or club soda

Squeeze of lemon juice

1 rosemary sprig or 1 lemon wheel

To a 4-ounce (120-ml) glass, add the gin, sweet vermouth, and Aperitivo Cappelletti. Stir briskly, then top it off with the tonic water and a squeeze of lemon. Garnish with a rosemary sprig or lemon wheel.

VARIATION
These are also a great batched cocktail. Increase the ingredients to 2 fl. ounces (60 ml) of gin and 1 fl. ounce (30 ml) each of vermouth and Cappelletti per serving, then multiply by however many servings you like. Top with tonic water, stir, then pour into ice-filled cocktail glasses, garnishing with rosemary sprigs or lemon wheels.

MAKE IT BEAUTIFUL Glassware is key here—I used tiny vintage cocktail glasses for the "tiny tonics," but you can increase the quantities to serve these in your prettiest cocktail glasses or Nick & Nora glasses.

AN ENGLISH TEA PARTY

An English tea party is the perfect excuse to bring out your finest dishes and tea service. This menu makes a great bridal or baby shower theme as well (and don't forget your fascinator!). **Serves 4 to 6**

Curried-Chicken Tea Sandwiches (page 46)
Cucumber-Herb Tea Sandwiches (page 46)
Currant-Cardamom Scones (page 47)

ACCOMPANIMENTS

Classic shortbread and colorful French macarons

Clotted cream or whipped cream

Lemon curd

Raspberry jam, strawberry jam, or orange marmalade

Major Grey's mango chutney, preferably Brooklyn Delhi (optional)

Seasonal berries, such as blueberries, blackberries, strawberries, and/or raspberries

Edible flowers, such as chamomile flowers and miniature English daisies

TO DRINK

An assortment of English teas, such as English breakfast or Earl Grey. Serve with milk, sugar cubes, and thinly sliced lemon according to your preference.

PUTTING IT TOGETHER

Use your best porcelain tea service and pretty platters for the sandwiches, scones, shortbread, and macarons. Place extra chutney in a small bowl next to the sandwiches. Offer sugar cubes in a small dish and milk in a small pitcher for the tea. Decorate the plated foods with edible flowers. Fill elegant little bowls (or even dainty teacups) with lemon curd, clotted cream, and jam, and add small spoons for serving. Arrange the fresh berries and lemon slices on small plates or in shallow bowls.

Curried-Chicken Tea Sandwiches

These sandwiches—a variation of classic coronation chicken salad, which was originally served at Queen Elizabeth II's coronation luncheon—include dried cherries, tarragon, and turmeric.

Makes 12 tea sandwiches

2 cups (390 g) chopped cooked chicken

⅓ cup (35 g) finely sliced celery

⅓ cup (75 ml) plus 1 tablespoon mayonnaise

2 teaspoons Dijon mustard

1 teaspoon Madras curry powder

½ teaspoon ground turmeric

Freshly ground black pepper

½ cup (75 g) chopped dried cherries

2 tablespoons finely chopped fresh tarragon

Kosher salt

8 slices white bread, crusts removed

¼ cup (60 ml) Major Grey's mango chutney

In a medium bowl, combine the chicken and celery. In a smaller bowl, whisk or stir together the mayonnaise, mustard, curry powder, turmeric, and pepper to taste. Pour over the chicken, stirring to combine. Fold in the cherries, tarragon, and salt to taste. Cover and refrigerate for 30 minutes.

For the sandwiches, spread a layer of chutney on half of the bread slices. Spread the chicken salad on top of the chutney. Top with the remaining bread slices. Cut the sandwiches into three even strips for finger sandwiches and serve.

MAKE IT BEAUTIFUL Clean the knife after each slice to make sure the edges of the sandwiches stay neat. Add edible mini daisies to the sandwich platter along with a small ramekin of extra mango chutney.

Cucumber-Herb Tea Sandwiches

I like using sliced brioche in these divine cucumber sandwiches, although any good-quality soft white bread will do.

Makes 12 finger sandwiches

8 ounces (225 g) cream cheese, at room temperature

2 tablespoons each finely chopped fresh dill and chives

Grated zest of 1 lemon

Garlic salt and freshly ground pepper

8 slices good-quality white bread, crusts removed

2 Persian cucumbers, peeled, thinly sliced, and patted dry with a paper towel

In a medium bowl, combine the cream cheese, herbs, lemon zest, garlic salt, and pepper to taste and stir to blend well. Using a small offset spatula or butter knife, coat each slice of bread with the cream cheese mixture. Arrange the cucumber slices slightly overlapping on top of the cream cheese and then sandwich together. Slice each sandwich into thirds and serve right away.

Currant–Cardamom Scones

These lovely scones have a delicate crumb and a slightly crusty exterior. Flavored and scented with cardamom and dotted with Zante currants, they're brushed with cream and sprinkled with turbinado sugar before baking to give them a crunchy texture.

Makes 6 to 8 small scones | Serves 4 to 6

2 cups (250 g) all-purpose flour, plus more for dusting

⅓ cup (65 g) sugar

1 tablespoon baking powder

1½ teaspoons ground cardamom

½ teaspoon kosher salt

½ cup (115 g) cold unsalted butter, preferably European style, cubed

½ cup (65 g) Zante currants

1 large egg

1½ teaspoons vanilla bean paste or vanilla extract

½ cup (120 ml) plus 2 tablespoons cold heavy cream

Grated zest of 1 lemon

2 tablespoons turbinado sugar, for sprinkling (optional)

Butter, jam, or lemon curd, for serving

In a large bowl, combine the 2 cups (250 g) flour, the sugar, baking powder, cardamom, and salt. Stir with a whisk to blend. Using your hands or a pastry cutter, cut the butter into the flour mixture until the butter is the size of peas. Add the currants and toss in the mixture until evenly combined.

In a small bowl, whisk the egg and vanilla bean paste with the ½ cup (120-ml) cream, then add the lemon zest. Make a well in the center of the dry ingredients and add the cream mixture. Mix the dough with your hands just until it holds together; don't overmix. On a lightly floured surface, form the dough into a 5½-inch (15-cm) disc about 1½ inches (4 cm) thick. Using a 2-inch (5 cm) round cutter, cut out 4 to 5 scones. Press together the scraps, press into a disk, and continue to cut out scones; you should get 6 to 8 total. Alternatively, cut the dough disc into 8 equal triangular wedges. Transfer the dough rounds to an airtight container, arranging them in a single layer, and refrigerate for at least 1 hour or up to overnight.

When ready to bake, preheat the oven to 400°F (205°C) and line a sheet pan with parchment paper. Brush the tops and sides of the scones with the remaining 2 tablespoons cream. Sprinkle each scone with turbinado sugar, if using. Arrange the scones on the sheet pan, spacing them about 1 inch (2.5 cm) apart.

Bake until the scones are golden brown, 17 to 18 minutes. Remove the scones from the oven and let cool on the sheet pan on a wire rack for 10 minutes; serve warm, halved and spread with butter, lemon curd, or jam. These are best if eaten the same day. Store in a container with a tight-fitting lid.

BAKING TIP
These are wonderful with dried blueberries or chopped dried cherries, just swap out the same amount of the currants. You can also swap out the cardamom for ground cinnamon.

GIRL'S DAY CHARCUTER-YAY BOARD

Sweet, salty, briny, and creamy—this classic board has something for everyone. Cured meats are served with several kinds of cheeses with different textures, such as one soft, one semi-soft and one semi-hard. Meats and cheeses are rounded out with seasonal and dried fruits, nuts, spreads, and pickles. An easy-to-make savory frico and a sweet brittle make this board even more satisfying. Add your own favorite ingredients to give this board your personal touch. This is ideal for a girl's day with your dearest friends. You can easily keep this board gluten-free by omitting the baguette slices and choosing gluten-free crackers. **Serves 4 to 6**

Parmesan Frico (page 50)
Cashew-Rosemary-Maple Brittle (page 51)

ACCOMPANIMENTS

Cured meats such as sliced salami and prosciutto

A variety of cheeses, such as aged goat cheese, a triple-cream cheese like Cowgirl Creamery's Mt. Tam, and Comté

Seasonal fruit, such as grapes, kumquats, berries, pears, or apples

Dried fruits, such as dried apricots and dried figs

Pickled vegetables and whole Castelvetrano olives

Marcona almonds or other toasted nuts

Grainy mustard, fig jam, and/or honey

Baguette slices and crackers

Edible flowers, such as rosemary flowers, plus rosemary sprigs and citrus leaves, for decorating (optional)

TO DRINK

Pinot Grigio or other light, dry white wine

PUTTING IT TOGETHER

If you are using a wheel of cheese, slice it in half and stack the halves on top of one another. Other cheeses can be sliced or artfully served. Arrange the cheeses and charcuterie on a large board, then fill in with fresh and dried fruits, adding the frico and brittle on the outer perimeter of the board. Fill small bowls with the pickled vegetables, olives, almonds, mustard, jam, and/or honey—and don't forget a few small spoons. Arrange these on and around the board. Decorate with the edible flowers for a gorgeous pop of color, plus the herb sprigs and citrus leaves. We used kumquat leaves, but you can also ask your local florist for a spray of salal leaves.

Parmesan Frico

One of the easiest, quickest, and simplest accompaniments to any charcuterie and or cheese board, this recipe has only one ingredient—Parmesan cheese—and takes only a few minutes to make. Buy the best wedge of imported Parmigiano Reggiano that you can afford and use a microplane to grate it just before making the frico.

Makes about 1 dozen | Serves 4

1 cup (100 g) grated Parmesan cheese

Preheat the oven to 400°F (205°C) and line a sheet pan with a Silpat or parchment paper. Using a Microplane, grate the Parmesan into a small bowl. Using a heaping tablespoonful of the grated cheese, place mounds of cheese 1 inch (2.5 cm) apart on the prepared sheet pan. Bake until lightly golden, 6 to 7 minutes, and then cool on the pan on a wire rack for 1 minute. Using an offset spatula, transfer the frico to a wire rack to cool completely. They will continue to crisp as they cool. These are best the day they are made. Store any leftovers in an airtight glass jar at room temperature.

BAKING TIP
Sprinkle with freshly cracked black pepper, finely chopped fresh rosemary, or red pepper flakes before baking for a delightful variation.

MAKE IT BEAUTIFUL Watch these carefully as they bake and don't let them get too dark. These rustic snacks will vary in shape which is part of their charm.

Cashew–Rosemary–Maple Brittle

A little something sweet is always a treat on a charcuterie and cheese board, whether it's a small drizzle of honey, a little bowl of fruity jam, or a sweet brittle like this one, which is made with chopped cashews, maple syrup, and brown sugar and flavored with fresh rosemary.

Makes one 8 x 6-inch (20 x 15-cm) sheet
Serves 6

1 cup (120 g) raw cashews, chopped

2 tablespoons plus 2 teaspoons pure Grade-A maple syrup

1 tablespoon finely chopped fresh rosemary

1 tablespoon packed light brown sugar

⅛ teaspoon kosher salt

Flaky salt, for finishing (optional)

MAKE IT BEAUTIFUL Decorate the plate of brittle with a sprig of unsprayed blossoming fresh rosemary if you can find it; if not, use regular rosemary sprigs.

Arrange an oven rack in the center of the oven and preheat the oven to 325°F (165°C). Line a small sheet pan with a Silpat baking mat or a double layer of parchment paper.

Put the chopped cashews in a fine-mesh sieve and sift over a sink several times to get rid of any too-small particles; You want all the cashew pieces to be fairly uniform in size. In a medium bowl, mix the cashews, maple syrup, rosemary, brown sugar, and kosher salt together using a rubber spatula until all the nut pieces are coated evenly.

Spoon the nut mixture onto the prepared sheet pan and use an offset spatula to press it into an 8 x 6-inch (20 x 15-cm) rectangle in the center of the pan. Bake until light amber in color, 15 to 18 minutes, rotating the pan every 5 minutes.

As soon as the pan comes out of the oven, sprinkle the brittle with flaky salt, if using, and place the sheet pan on a wire rack. If the edges of the brittle are darker, trim them with a small knife while the brittle is warm. Let cool for about 20 minutes; the brittle will harden as it cools. Break into shards and serve.

NEW MEXICAN NACHO BOARD

In New Mexico, enchiladas and other dishes are ordered either red, green, or "Christmas," which means with both red and green sauces. These "Christmas-style" nachos are a colorful and fun way to serve a group of friends any time of year. Here, I use my homemade red salsa and a store-bought Hatch green chile salsa to dress up these sheet pan nachos, and pay homage to my hometown: Albuquerque, New Mexico. Serves 4 to 6

Quick & Easy Salsa (page 54)
Red & Green Chile Fiesta Nachos (page 55)

ACCOMPANIMENTS
Hatch green chile salsa
Sliced fresh jalapeños or pickled jalapeño slices, drained
Canned sliced black olives, drained
Fresh cilantro sprigs
Fresh avocado slices
Mexican crema or sour cream
Chile-limón seasoning and lime wedges

TO DRINK
Store-bought canned lime margaritas, served on the rocks with a chile-limón seasoning rim, and/or Strawberry Hibiscus Margaritas (page 99)

PUTTING IT TOGETHER
Serve the nachos on the same sheet pan they were assembled and baked on. Dress them up with the salsas, sliced jalapeños, olives, cilantro, and avocado slices. Put additional salsa, jalapeños, olives, avocado, and crema in separate bowls alongside the nachos. I also like to include an extra bowl of chips for everyone to use for dipping. Additionally, set out a plate of cilantro, chile-limón seasoning, and lime wedges for guests who want to add more to their nachos and refresh their margaritas.

Quick & Easy Salsa

This quick, homemade salsa has a smoky heat thanks to the chipotle chiles. Fresh lime zest and juice bring acidity and brightness, cumin adds warmth, and fresh jalapeños and New Mexico chile powder add a little more heat. I use garlic salt in this recipe; however, remember that the tortilla chips will be salty, so be sure to taste.

Makes 1²/₃ cups (405 ml) | Serves 4

One 14½-ounce (415-g) can fire-roasted tomatoes with chipotle chiles, with their juices

⅓ cup (15 g) finely chopped fresh cilantro, plus more for garnish (optional)

¼ cup (30 g) chopped shallots

½ jalapeño, seeded and finely diced

3 small cloves garlic, sliced

¾ teaspoon dried oregano, preferably Mexican

½ teaspoon medium or hot red chile powder, preferably New Mexico chile powder

¼ teaspoon ground cumin

¼ teaspoon garlic salt or kosher salt

Grated zest and juice of 1 lime

In a small food processor, combine all the ingredients and pulse until your desired consistency. Add salt to taste. Serve the salsa in a small bowl and garnish with a sprig or two of cilantro, if desired. Refrigerate leftover salsa in an airtight jar for up to 1 week or freeze for up to 1 year.

RECIPE TIP
If you aren't a cilantro fan, simply just leave it out. Some people, like my husband, have variation in the OR6A2 gene that gives cilantro a soapy taste when eaten.

MAKE IT BEAUTIFUL Add a few sprigs of fresh cilantro as a garnish to your bowl of salsa.

Red & Green Chile Fiesta Nachos

These "Christmas-style" nachos are an homage to my hometown of Albuquerque, New Mexico. Serve them hot from the oven with their melty cheese and dressed up with Hatch green chile salsa from Hatch, New Mexico, and homemade red salsa made with New Mexico chile powder and smoky chipotle chiles. Accompany with one, more, or all of the optional toppings.

Serves 4 to 6

One 12-ounce (340-g) bag tortilla chips

3 cups (345 g) shredded mild Cheddar or Monterey Jack cheese, or a mixture

¼ cup (60 ml) Quick & Easy Salsa (opposite)

¼ cup (60 ml) Hatch green chile salsa or green salsa of your choice

❧❧❧

Toppings and Garnishes (optional)

One 2¼-ounce (65-g) can sliced black olives, drained

1 jalapeño, sliced or ¼ cup (60 g) sliced pickled jalapeños, drained

1 ripe avocado, pitted, peeled, and sliced

¼ cup (60 ml) Mexican crema or sour cream

Fresh cilantro sprigs, for garnish

1 lime, cut into small wedges

Arrange an oven rack in the center of the oven and preheat the oven to 350°F (175°C). Spread the tortilla chips on a rimmed sheet pan and sprinkle with the cheese. Bake until the cheese is melted and bubbling, 10 to 12 minutes. Top the nachos evenly with the Quick & Easy Salsa and Hatch green chile salsa and serve with some or all of the suggested toppings, with the limes alongside for squeezing.

RECIPE TIP
Use sturdy rather than thin chips here so they will hold up under the toppings. Feel free to swap in your favorite toppings, such as guacamole; cooked, taco-seasoned ground meat; warmed refried, whole pinto, or black beans; or shredded pepper Jack cheese.

MAKE IT BEAUTIFUL *Blue corn is a staple in New Mexico and will give these nachos a vibrant Southwestern spin. If you can find blue corn tortilla chips for this recipe, they would make these nachos extra beautiful.*

A COBB SALAD FOR SHARING

Julie & Julia is one of my most revered movies of all time. Two of my favorite scenes in the movie are when Julie tells her husband she's dreading having lunch with her friends the next day, "Ritual Cobb salad lunch tomorrow, dreading, dreading, dreading." During the lunch, they each order a Cobb salad with a request to leave off one specific ingredient: "Cobb salad no blue cheese, Cobb salad no beets, Cobb salad no bacon, Cobb salad no egg." And Julie is chastised for eating a breadstick! In this recipe, I don't hold back on any of these ingredients, and the salad is accompanied by Julia Child-inspired herbes de Provence grissini (thin, crunchy breadsticks). I wouldn't hesitate to serve this for a girl's day birthday luncheon. **Serves 4 to 6**

Cobb Salad (page 58)
Smoky Blue Cheese Dressing (page 59)
Herbes de Provence Grissini (page 60)

ACCOMPANIMENTS
Thinly sliced fresh chives and crushed pink peppercorns, for garnish
Edible flowers, such as rose geraniums (optional)

TO DRINK
Hibiscus iced tea with lemon or sparkling rosé

PUTTING IT TOGETHER
Serve this on the nicest sheet pan or platter that you have; I used my Great Jones raspberry-colored coated ceramic sheet pan for this presentation. Put the dressing in a couple of bowls (for easy sharing), garnish with crushed pink peppercorns and fresh chives, and add small serving spoons alongside. Add a tiny dish of extra pink peppercorns to brighten and flavor the salad. (Hand-crush or gently crush the pink peppercorns in a mortar and pestle; don't put them in a spice grinder.) I also set out pink salt and a cute pepper mill to add more vibrancy to this scene. Place the grissini in a breadbasket. I love adding flowers—set out a small bud vase of pink straw flowers on the table for an added burst of color. Decorate with the edible flowers if you like. Here, I used rose geraniums for their vivid pink hue; the flowers and leaves are both edible.

Cobb Salad

Gather your girlfriends and share this giant family-style salad—no cell phones allowed. It has something for everyone, including golden beets, wedges of blue cheese, sliced avocados, crispy bacon, and hard-cooked eggs. Leave out the bacon for a vegetarian version, or, for a heartier salad, add shredded or sliced cooked rotisserie chicken.

Serves 4 to 6

1 head green or red butter lettuce, 2 or 3 heads Little Gem lettuces, or 2 heads baby romaine, separated into leaves

6-ounce (170-g) wedge of smoky or regular blue cheese, halved lengthwise

8 slices crisp-cooked bacon

3 hard-boiled eggs, peeled and halved (see page 64)

1 to 2 avocados, pitted, peeled, and sliced

1 cup (145 g) cherry tomatoes

8 pickled golden or red beets, sliced

Salt and freshly ground black pepper

Minced fresh chives and crushed pink peppercorns, for garnish (optional)

Edible flowers, such as rose geraniums, for garnish (optional)

Smoky Blue Cheese Dressing (opposite)

Arrange the lettuce leaves in an even layer on a rimmed sheet pan. Place the blue cheese wedges, bacon, eggs, avocado slices, and cherry tomatoes decoratively and in separate mounds on top of the lettuce. Add the beets to a small bowl for each guest to add as they wish.

Season the salad ingredients with salt and pepper. Garnish with the chives, pink peppercorns, and edible flowers, if using. Pass the blue cheese dressing alongside.

Smoky Blue Cheese Dressing

Smoked blue cheese adds warm flavor to this dressing, while lemon zest and lemon juice add a tangy note. The pink peppercorns lend both sweetness and vivid color. This dressing works really well on other salads too. You can also use a regular, creamy blue cheese for a milder, non-smoky version.

Makes 1 cup (240 ml) | Serves 4

⅓ cup (75 ml) plus 1 tablespoon sour cream

2 tablespoons mayonnaise

Grated zest of 1 lemon

1 tablespoon plus 2 teaspoons fresh lemon juice

2 tablespoons thinly sliced fresh chives

1 tablespoon buttermilk

½ cup (70 g) finely crumbled smoky blue cheese

Garlic salt, if needed

1½ teaspoons pink peppercorns, crushed

In a small bowl, combine the sour cream, mayonnaise, lemon zest and juice, chives, and buttermilk. Fold in the blue cheese and taste to see if you need salt; if so, add garlic salt to taste. Add the crushed pink peppercorns. Store the dressing in a glass jar with a tight-fitting lid in the refrigerator for up to 1 week.

MAKE IT BEAUTIFUL *Pink peppercorns are vibrant and flavorful in this dressing, so try to seek them out. Also, add plenty of fresh chives as well.*

Herbes de Provence Grissini

Italian grissini are crunchy, pen-sized breadsticks that are terrific for snacking when served with cheese and olives, and they're brilliant alongside a huge, shareable salad. Often seasoned with flaky salt, Parmesan, seeds, or dried herbs, here they're made with herbes de Provence. Julia Child is credited with introducing American home cooks to this herbaceous blend of dried oregano, summer savory, thyme, and rosemary.

Makes 24 grissini | Serves 6 to 8

½ teaspoon active dry yeast

½ cup (125 ml) warm (110°F/43°C) water

1¼ cups (155 g) all-purpose flour

2 tablespoons bread flour

1¼ teaspoons herbes de Provence

1¼ teaspoons kosher salt

2 tablespoons olive oil, plus more for brushing

Flaky salt for sprinkling (optional)

In a small bowl, whisk the yeast into the warm water and let stand until foamy, about 5 minutes. In the bowl of a stand mixer, whisk together the flours, herbes de Provence, and salt.

Using the dough hook, add the yeast mixture and the 2 tablespoons olive oil. Mix on low speed until all the flour is incorporated. Turn the dough out onto a lightly floured work surface and knead for 5 minutes.

Oil a medium bowl or the stand mixer bowl and add the dough, turning it once to coat with oil. Cover with a clean towel and let stand in a warm place until doubled in size, about 1 hour.

Line two sheet pans with parchment paper and preheat the oven to 375°F (190°C). On a lightly floured surface, divide the dough into 24 equal pieces. Using your hands, roll the dough pieces into ropes about 8 inches (20 cm) long.

Place 12 grissini 1 inch (2.5 cm) apart on each of the prepared baking sheets. Brush the grissini with olive oil and sprinkle evenly with flaky salt, if using. Bake one sheet at a time, keeping the unbaked grissini covered with a towel.

Bake until golden brown, 20 to 22 minutes. Cool the grissini on a wire rack leaving them on the pans until completely cooled; they will crisp as they cool. Serve immediately, or store in an airtight container for up to 4 days.

BAKING TIP
If your shaped grissini shrink before baking, let them rest and stretch again right before brushing them with oil and putting them in the oven.

MAKE IT BEAUTIFUL *Serve these in a bread basket or in a large glass to show them off on your table.*

UKRAINIAN BUDMO BOARD

This menu, contributed by my good friend Anna Voloshyna—a Ukrainian chef, teacher, and cookbook author—celebrates some of her country's favorite foods: mushrooms and fresh cherries. BUDMO!, the name of Anna's cookbook, means "cheers" and is a favorite toast in Ukraine. We shopped together for many of the accompaniments on this board at a specialty shop called Royal Market in San Francisco; look for these specialty ingredients at Eastern European markets or online. This board is dedicated to the people and the resilience of Ukraine. **Serves 4 to 6**

Beet-Pickled Deviled Eggs (page 64)
Mushroom & Green Lentil Pâté (page 65)

ACCOMPANIMENTS
Thinly sliced dark rye bread
Ajvar (red bell pepper dip)
Marinated tomatoes
Dill pickles
Fresh sour or sweet cherries
Salo (cured fatback)
Fresh herbs, such as sliced chives and dill, chervil, and/or oregano sprigs

TO DRINK
Ice-cold cherry or regular vodka

PUTTING IT TOGETHER
Both mushrooms and cherries are beloved in Ukrainian cuisine. Serve this colorful menu in the late spring or summer, when fresh cherries are in season. Arrange the rye bread slices on a small wooden board and set next to the dish of pâté; garnish the pâté with a sprig of fresh oregano. Add the ajvar dip to a small bowl and set next to the rye bread and pâté. Place the beet-pickled deviled eggs on a beautiful plate and garnish them with minced chives and a spray or two of fresh dill and chervil. Put the marinated tomatoes, dill pickles, and cherries in bowls. Place the salo on a small chilled plate, keeping it cold until ready to serve; sprinkle with fresh chives. Toast each other with cherry vodka in your most elegant glasses and say, "budmo!"

Beet–Pickled Deviled Eggs

Infused with the piquant kick of horseradish, these eye–catching, magenta–hued eggs are a staple on cookbook author Anna Voloshyna's table. The striking color is achieved by pickling the eggs in a mixture of beet juice, white vinegar, raw beets, and black peppercorns for up to 3 days. If you can't find natural beet juice, just use the liquid from a can of cooked beets.

Serves 4 to 6

8 large eggs

1 cup (240 ml) natural beet juice

½ cup (120 ml) plus 1 tablespoon distilled white vinegar

⅓ cup (45 g) peeled and thinly sliced raw red beet

1 garlic clove

2 tablespoons sugar

2 teaspoons kosher salt

½ teaspoon black peppercorns

~~~

Filling

8 hard-boiled egg yolks (above)

¼ cup (60 ml) mayonnaise

1 tablespoon prepared horseradish sauce

1 tablespoon mustard powder

Kosher salt and freshly ground black pepper

~~~

1 tablespoon minced fresh chives, for garnish

Dill and or chervil sprigs, for garnish (optional)

Flaky salt, for sprinkling (optional)

To hard-boil the eggs, place the eggs in a large saucepan and add cold water to cover by about 1 inch (2.5 cm). Bring to a full boil over high heat, then remove the pan from the heat. Cover and let the eggs sit undisturbed for 12 minutes. Drain and rinse the eggs with cold water, then transfer to a bowl of ice water until cool enough to handle. Peel the eggs, discarding the peel, and set aside.

In the saucepan, combine 1 cup (240 ml) water, the beet juice, vinegar, sliced beet, garlic, sugar, salt, and peppercorns. Bring to a boil over high heat, reduce the heat to low and simmer for 10 minutes. Remove from the heat and let cool for 5 minutes. Put the eggs in a large, wide-mouthed glass jar and pour the hot brine mixture over the eggs; they should be covered. Let the brine cool to room temperature, then cap the jar tightly and refrigerate the eggs for at least 24 hours before filling and serving. The eggs will keep in the brine for up to 3 days. (The longer they are in the brine, the deeper the color will be; I usually brine them for 2 days.)

When ready to fill the eggs, remove the eggs and set aside, discarding the brine mixture. Cut the eggs in half lengthwise and remove the yolks, reserving the pink egg white halves.

To make the filling, in a small bowl or a small food processor or blender (use a food processor or blender if you plan to pipe the filling) combine the egg yolks, mayonnaise, horseradish sauce, and mustard powder. Mash with a fork or process until smooth. Season to taste with salt and pepper.

Arrange the pink egg white halves, hollow side up, on a work surface. Spoon or pipe the yolk mixture into the egg white halves using a pastry bag. Serve, topped with chives, dill, and/or chervil, and sprinkled with flaky salt, if using.

Mushroom & Green Lentil Pâté

Mushrooms are an important ingredient in Ukrainian cuisine, from soups to savory pies. This mushroom pâté is an elegant vegetarian appetizer for a fancy dinner party. The combination of earthy mushrooms, hearty green lentils, and fragrant shallots is elevated by the addition of Madeira and oregano, resulting in a pâté that is both savory and slightly sweet. Butter and heavy cream give it a richness that pairs perfectly with dark rye bread.

Makes 2 cups (480 ml) | Serves 6 to 8

⅓ cup (65 g) French green lentils, rinsed, preferably Puy

1⅓ cups (315 ml) vegetable stock, plus more if needed

3 tablespoons unsalted butter

1 tablespoon sunflower or canola oil

1 large shallot, coarsely chopped

1 pound (455 g) assorted fresh mushrooms such as cremini, stemmed shiitake, and oyster, cleaned, dried, and coarsely chopped

½ cup (120 ml) Madeira

1 teaspoon chopped fresh oregano

2 tablespoons heavy cream

½ teaspoon kosher salt

Freshly ground black pepper

In a small saucepan, combine the lentils and vegetable stock. Bring to a boil, then reduce the heat to a simmer and cook until the lentils are tender, 20 to 25 minutes. If all the liquid evaporates before the lentils are fully cooked, add a bit more.

In a large saucepan, melt the butter with sunflower oil over medium heat. Add the chopped shallot and cook until translucent, about 3 minutes.

Add the chopped mushrooms and stir to coat with the butter and shallot mixture. Cook for 10 to 15 minutes, stirring occasionally, until the mushrooms release their liquid and are tender and browned.

Add the Madeira and oregano to the pan and cook until the liquid has reduced by about half, 5 or 10 more minutes. Remove from the heat and let cool.

Transfer the mixture to a blender and add the lentils and cream. Process until smooth. Season with the salt and pepper to taste. If the mixture is too thick, add a splash more or two of heavy cream or stock to thin it out.

Transfer the mushroom pâté to a serving dish and chill in the refrigerator for at least 2 hours or up to overnight before serving. Serve with dense rye bread and other accompaniments.

MAKE IT BEAUTIFUL *Save a few thinly sliced raw mushrooms to garnish the top of the pâté along with a sprig of oregano.*

PICNIC IN THE PARK

On warm days, my husband and I walk over to San Francisco's Golden Gate Park—which is practically our backyard—and have a picnic with friends on the lawn at the Conservatory of Flowers. Pasta salad and mini tuna and olive salad sandwiches, along with fresh fruit and store-bought cookies, are our favorite picnic offerings, but you can pick and choose among these and add your own favorite alfresco foods. I like to make it a little fancy by including small drinking glasses, my favorite pasta salad bowl, a table linen, colorful melamine plates, and a pretty melamine board to place everything on. **Serves 4 to 6**

Campanelle Pasta Salad (page 68)
Mini Tuna–Olive Salad Sandwiches (page 71)

ACCOMPANIMENTS
Seasonal fresh fruit, such as fresh figs, Concord or red grapes, strawberries,
  or sliced stone fruits
Pimiento-stuffed olives speared with frilly toothpicks
Store-bought cookies

TO DRINK
Bottled French lemonade with slices of lemon

PUTTING IT TOGETHER
Whether you gather in a city park, by a country stream, or in your own backyard, pack your picnic basket with a melamine board and plates, drinkware, and cutlery, as well as one of your favorite table linens. Pack the tuna salad filling, sprouts or lettuce, bread, and speared olives separately and build the sandwiches alfresco, right before serving. Pack the pasta salad in an airtight container or your favorite bowl (well covered) and toss in a gel ice pack or two. Also, take along a little extra dressing to add just before serving. Store a bag of ice alongside the lemonade in a small cooler. Bring the fruit in a little basket and keep the cookies in their wrapping until you serve. We added pretty orange nasturtium flowers to smarten up this picnic scene.

Campanelle Pasta Salad

This pasta salad is not only ideal for a picnic, but great for any alfresco meal: potlucks, the beach, or a barbecue. Use any favorite short, sturdy pasta shape, like campanelle ("bellflower" in Italian), rotini, or cavatappi—you want a pasta with lots of nooks and crannies to catch all the dressing. Castelvetrano olives and feta cheese are both salty, so taste the salad before adding salt. Don't rinse the artichokes and sundried tomatoes, the oils lend great flavor to the salad. This is a terrific make-ahead recipe that I know you will love!

Serves 4 to 6

Honey-Balsamic Dressing

¼ cup (60 ml) balsamic vinegar

¼ cup (60 ml) Dijon mustard, regular or grainy

¼ cup (60 ml) olive oil

¼ cup (60 ml) raw wildflower honey

¼ teaspoon Italian seasoning

¼ teaspoon red pepper flakes (optional)

—

½ pound (225 g) dried small pasta shapes such as campanelle, rotini, or cavatappi

Olive oil, for drizzling

¾ cup (115 g) crumbled feta

½ cup (55 g) julienned oil-packed sun-dried tomatoes, drained

½ cup (70 g) packed Castelvetrano olives or other green olives, pitted and halved

½ cup (128 g) drained marinated artichoke hearts, sliced

3 tablespoons minced fresh flat-leaf parsley, plus more for garnish (optional)

3 tablespoons minced fresh basil, plus more for garnish (optional)

Kosher salt and freshly ground black pepper

To make the dressing, in a medium jar, combine the balsamic vinegar, mustard, olive oil, honey, Italian seasoning, and red pepper flakes, if using. Close with a tight-fitting lid and shake vigorously until emulsified. Use immediately, or refrigerate for up to 2 weeks.

Cook the pasta in a large pot of salted boiling water until al dente according to the package directions. Drain and toss with a little olive oil.

Pour ½ cup (120 ml) of the dressing into a large bowl, add the warm pasta, and gently toss to coat; let cool to room temperature, about 15 minutes. Add the feta, sun-dried tomatoes, olives, artichoke hearts, the 3 tablespoons parsley, and the 3 tablespoons basil. Toss to mix and season to taste with salt and pepper. Cover and refrigerate for 1 hour before serving. If desired, garnish with more parsley and basil. Serve with extra dressing on the side, if needed.

COOKING TIP
To make this for a potluck lunch to serve on its own, I sometimes add ½ pound (225 g) salami, cut into matchsticks.

MAKE IT BEAUTIFUL Reserve a little of each ingredient to place decoratively on the bowls after serving. Keep the extra herbs, if using to garnish, in a small jar with water so that they stay fresh to adorn your pasta salad.

Mini Tuna–Olive Salad Sandwiches

These extra-flavorful sandwiches are great for picnics. The pickled jalapeños add a kick, the celery adds texture, and the olives and sun-dried tomatoes take tuna salad to a new level. I call it my "everything but the kitchen sink" tuna salad.

Makes 4 sandwiches | Serves 4 to 6

Two (5-ounce/142 g) cans solid white albacore tuna in water, drained well and flaked

½ cup (75 g) pimiento-stuffed olives, drained and thinly sliced or chopped

¼ cup (26 g) oil-packed sun-dried tomatoes, drained, patted dry, and finely chopped

¼ cup (25 g) thinly sliced celery

¼ cup (20 g) finely chopped celery leaves

¼ cup (13 g) finely chopped fresh dill

2 tablespoons finely chopped pickled jalapeño

2 tablespoons thinly sliced fresh chives

Grated zest of ½ lemon

2 teaspoons fresh lemon juice

¼ cup (60 ml) mayonnaise

1 teaspoon Dijon mustard

Garlic salt

Freshly ground black pepper

Pinch of red pepper flakes (optional)

8 slices whole-wheat or sourdough bread

Sprouts or lettuce leaves

Whole pimiento-stuffed olives, for spearing (optional)

In a medium bowl, combine the tuna, olives, sun-dried tomatoes, celery, celery leaves, dill, jalapeño, chives, and lemon zest and juice. Using a rubber spatula, mix all the ingredients together. Add the mayonnaise and Dijon and mix well. Season to taste with the garlic salt and pepper and add the red pepper flakes, if using.

To assemble, line half of the bread slices with the sprouts or lettuce. Spread evenly with the tuna salad and top with the remaining bread slices. Cut the sandwiches into halves or quarters and spear each portion with a pimiento-stuffed olive on a toothpick.

RECIPE TIPS

Use a sturdy bread for these sandwiches and put them together right before enjoying. I like to cut the crusts off, but that is optional. Feel free to swap out the pimiento-stuffed olives for your most-loved variety.

MAKE IT BEAUTIFUL *Look for frilly multicolored-cellophane toothpicks to spear the olives for these sandwiches.*

HAPPY HOUR

The boards in this chapter, filled with nibbles and finger foods, are brought to life with lively cocktails—perfect pairings for after work libations or casual gatherings with friends. From aperitivos and apéritifs to martinis and margaritas, there is a glass of something delightful here to get the party started. And don't forget these cocktails that appear with other boards in the book: Strawberry Hibiscus Margaritas (page 99), Italian Gin & Tonics (page 43), Cappelletti Spritzes (page 76), and classic prosecco. If you don't drink alcohol, there are many whimsical and delectable nonalcoholic beverages on the market, such as Ghia spritzes, Drømme, and St. Agrestis. There are also nonalcoholic versions of classic distilled spirits, including bourbon, gin, vodka, and tequila that you can use in place of the real thing in any of these cocktail recipes.

APERITIVO TIME

An aperitivo is a pre-dinner drink in Italy. My first encounter with one was a beautiful orange Aperol spritz served to me in a balloon glass in Rome. Since then, I've expanded my drinks repertoire to include several other brilliantly colored, vibrant cocktails, perfect to serve with salty snacks before any meal, like the spiced almonds and citrus-infused olives in this menu.
Serves 4 to 6

Cappelletti Spritz (page 76)
Italian Spiced Almonds (page 76)
Clementine–Rosemary Olives (page 77)

ACCOMPANIMENTS
Salumi (cured meats), such as sliced soppressata and salami
Italian cheeses, such as marinated mozzarella balls and a wedge of Parmesan
Sliced ciabatta bread, taralli (Italian crackers), and/or potato chips
Red seedless grapes
Caperberries
Fresh herb sprigs, for garnish (optional)

TO DRINK
Cappelletti Spritz

PUTTING IT TOGETHER
Arrange the salumi, cheeses, bread, and grapes on a board; if using fresh mozzarella balls, place them in a bowl on the board. Break the Parmesan cheese into shards with a cheese knife. Put the almonds, olives, taralli, and caperberries in small serving bowls. Garnish the board with herb sprigs for a fresh display.

Cappelletti Spritz

This brilliant red spritz is made with Aperitivo Cappelletti, an Italian bitters.

Makes 1 drink

1½ fl. ounces (45 ml) Aperitivo
Cappelletti

3 fl. ounces (90 ml) prosecco

1 fl. ounce (30 ml) San Pellegrino
sparkling water

1 lemon slice or wheel, for garnish

Fill a red wine or Nick & Nora glass with ice. Add the Cappelletti and prosecco and stir gently to blend. Top off with the San Pellegrino and garnish with a lemon slice or wheel.

MAKE IT BEAUTIFUL Use a microfiber polishing cloth to get rid of any water spots on your freshly washed and dried glassware.

Italian Spiced Almonds

Flavored with fresh rosemary, garlic, and Calabrian chile powder, these spicy nuts are finished with flaky salt. Wrapped in a bag secured with ribbon and a sprig or two of rosemary, these make a lovely gift for a host.

Makes 1½ cups (210 g) | Serves 4

1½ tablespoons olive oil

1 tablespoon finely chopped fresh
rosemary, plus 1 sprig, for garnish
(optional)

¾ to 1 teaspoon garlic salt

½ teaspoon hot Calabrian chile
powder or chili powder of your
choice

½ teaspoon Italian seasoning

⅛ teaspoon garlic powder

1½ cups (210 g) raw whole almonds

Flaky salt, for sprinkling (optional)

Line a small sheet pan with parchment paper and preheat the oven to 350°F (175°C).

In a medium bowl, combine the olive oil, rosemary, garlic salt, chile powder, Italian seasoning, and garlic powder and stir with a rubber spatula to blend. Add the almonds and toss to coat. Spread out in an even layer onto the prepared sheet pan, being sure to add all the spicy and salty oil, and roast for 15 minutes, giving the pan a shake every 5 minutes to make sure the nuts cook evenly.

Remove the almonds from the oven and sprinkle them on the pan with flaky salt, tossing them once more. Spread them in an even layer on the pan and place it on a wire rack. Let cool to room temperature, about 20 minutes. Store in an airtight glass jar for up to 2 weeks. Serve sprinkled with flaky salt and garnished with a rosemary sprig, if you like.

RECIPE TIP To check the doneness of the almonds, cut one in half with a paring knife. If it's tan on the inside, it is perfectly roasted. This works every time, thank you to my friend Kate!

Clementine-Rosemary Olives

These citrusy, herby olives are a lovely flavor complement to the slightly bitter, fruity flavor of aperitivos. If you can find clementines or tangerines, their flavor really shines here, though a Valencia or Cara Cara orange is equally as good. This recipe calls for Castelvetrano olives, though Cerignola olives are also nice. Look for a clementine–infused olive oil or other citrus olive oil. You can also substitute fresh oregano for the rosemary.

Makes 1¼ cups (195 g) | Serves 4

¼ cup (60 ml) clementine, citrus, or fruity olive oil

5 or 6 clementine or tangerine zest strips, plus more for garnish (optional)

1 large rosemary sprig or fresh oregano sprig, plus more for garnish (optional)

1 dried bay leaf

1 large or 3 small cloves garlic

1¼ cups (195 g) whole or pitted Castelvetrano olives, drained well and patted dry

MAKE IT BEAUTIFUL Serve in a bowl with a few more citrus strips and rosemary sprigs.

In a small saucepan, combine the olive oil, the 5 or 6 clementine zest strips, rosemary sprig, bay leaf, and garlic and cook over medium heat until the strips, rosemary, and garlic become fragrant and start to brown, 1 to 2 minutes; watching carefully to keep from burning.

Remove the pan from the heat and add the olives. Let stand for at least 30 minutes, swirling the pan occasionally.

Remove the rosemary sprig and bay leaf. You can leave the zest strips and garlic in if not too dark for serving.

Pour the olives and the oil into a small bowl and garnish with a fresh zest strip and a fresh rosemary sprig, if you like. Serve immediately or refrigerate in an airtight container for up to 1 week. Bring to room temperature or rewarm before serving.

COOKING TIP
Use the remaining oil from these olives to drizzle over salads and pizzas or to dip bread in.

FRENCH APÉRO HOUR

In France, the cocktail hour is known as the apéro, short for apéritif. My friend Eric Lundy, a chef, food stylist, and truly a bon viveur who specializes in French food, created this menu. His gin-based spritzes, rich pork and chicken liver terrine, and Quick-Pickled Shallots (page 81) make a beautiful board to serve with your best French Champagne or other sparkling wine. **Serves 4 to 6**

Pineau Spritz (page 80)
Terrine de Campagne (page 80)
Quick-Pickled Shallots (page 81)

ACCOMPANIMENTS

Lemon or salal leaves

French cheeses, 2 or 3 varieties, such as an ash-coated goat cheese, Comté, and Époisses

Crostini (page 108) or baguette slices

Cornichons

Grainy Dijon mustard

Herbed roasted cashews

French radishes, trimmed with about 1 to 2 inches (2.5 to 5 cm) of tops remaining, served with salted butter and flaky salt

Edible flowers and fresh herb sprigs, such as flowering thyme sprigs

TO DRINK

Pineau Spritz, Champagne, or other sparkling wine

PUTTING IT TOGETHER

Use a long, slender, elegant board for this one. Arrange the salal or lemon leaves on the board and place the sliced terrine and the French cheeses on the leaves. Leave any remaining terrine that doesn't fit on the board in the terrine dish and set aside if you need to replenish. Place the crostini alongside the board on a plate or a piece of parchment paper. Use small bowls for the pickled shallots, cornichons, mustard, and cashews. Put the radishes on a small board or plate with a small ramekin of salted butter and a pinch bowl of flaky salt. Finish the board with edible flowering thyme sprigs. For a bit of whimsy, include paper cocktail napkins and vintage transferware appetizer plates. Garnish the board with your favorite herbs and/or edible flowers to make this très chic!

MAKE IT BEAUTIFUL If you don't live in an area where lemon trees or salal shrubs grow, check with your local florist. Salal branches, with their shiny green leaves, are routinely used in bouquets.

Pineau Spritz

Here is Eric's recipe for a French apéritif using Pineau des Charentes, a fortified wine from the Poitou-Charentes region of France. He adds gin, a homemade honey syrup, Meyer lemon juice, and sparkling wine. This is great for a party, as it can easily be batched out. Just make sure to add the sparkling wine at the last minute.

Makes 1 drink

Honey Syrup

⅓ cup (80 ml) honey

¼ cup (60 ml) water

⟿

1½ fl. ounces (45 ml) Pineau des Charentes

1 fl. ounce (30 ml) gin

1 tablespoon fresh Meyer or regular lemon juice

1 tablespoon Honey Syrup (above)

A few dashes of orange bitters such as Angostura

2 to 3 fl. ounces (60 to 90 ml) sparkling wine

1 wide Meyer lemon or regular lemon zest strip

For the honey syrup: In a small saucepan, combine the honey and water. Stir over medium heat until the honey is dissolved, about 2 minutes. Let cool and then transfer to an airtight container. Store in the refrigerator for up to 1 month.

Add the Pineau des Charentes, gin, lemon juice, honey syrup, and bitters to a cocktail shaker filled with ice. Cover and shake vigorously.

Strain into an ice-filled champagne coupe and top with sparkling wine. Garnish with the lemon zest strip.

MAKE IT BEAUTIFUL You could also use a highball glass for this cocktail as well as a coupe.

Quatre Épices

This French blend of four spices is also a wonderful holiday baking mix for cakes and cookies.

Makes 4½ tablespoons

1½ tablespoons freshly ground nutmeg

1 tablespoon ground white pepper

1 tablespoon ground ginger

1 tablespoon ground cloves

In a small bowl, stir all the spices together. Store in a small jar with a tight-fitting lid for up to 6 months.

Quick-Pickled Shallots

Quick-pickled shallots are instant flavor bombs for any menu. These are steeped with red pepper flakes, fennel seeds, and pink peppercorns and are perfect with this menu as well as with the Pescatarian Challah Bagel Brunch (page 24). They're also great on a burger or sandwich, in a grain bowl, or added to salads and dressings.

Makes about 1¼ cups (190 g) | Serves 4 to 6

2 to 3 shallots, peeled and thinly sliced

2 teaspoons kosher salt

2 teaspoons sugar

½ cup (120 ml) Champagne vinegar or white wine vinegar

Pinch of red pepper flakes, crushed

¼ teaspoon fennel seeds

¼ teaspoon pink peppercorns

In a medium bowl, combine the shallots and 1 teaspoon *each* of the salt and sugar. Use your fingertips to gently massage the salt and sugar well throughout the shallot slices until the salt and sugar mixture dissolves and starts to draw liquid out of the shallot slices, about 30 seconds. Set aside while you prepare the pickling liquid.

In a small saucepan, combine the vinegar and ½ cup (120 ml) water along with the remaining 1 teaspoon *each* salt and sugar. Bring to a simmer over medium-high heat until the sugar and salt completely dissolve, 2 to 3 minutes. Remove from the heat and let cool for 2 to 3 minutes.

Put the rubbed shallot slices in a clean pint jar and add the pepper flakes, fennel seeds, and pink peppercorns. Pour the pickling liquid over the shallot slices. Let cool to room temperature, about 20 minutes, then refrigerate for at least 15 minutes or up to 24 hours before serving.

Store the remainder in a jar with a tight-fitting lid in the refrigerator for up to 2 weeks.

Terrine de Campagne

A terrine de campagne is a loaf made from various coarsely ground meats, herbs, and Cognac or brandy. For added texture it is studded with pistachios. The word *campagne* means "country" and distinguishes this rustic loaf from smooth-textured pâtés. Chef Eric Lundy notes that the terrine should be made one day ahead of serving but that, if well wrapped and refrigerated, it will keep for up to a week. He also recommends using a Le Creuset terrine pan. Serve this with slices of bread or Crostini (page 108), grainy Dijon mustard, Quick-Pickled Shallots (page 81), and cornichons.

Makes 1 terrine | Serves 12

3 tablespoons unsalted butter, plus more for the pan

1 cup (125 g) finely chopped white onion

¼ cup (60 ml) Cognac or brandy

1 cup (80 g) panko (Japanese bread crumbs)

¼ cup (60 ml) plus 2 tablespoons heavy cream

1 pound (455 g) ground fatty pork (80/20)

½ pound (225 g) chicken livers, coarsely chopped

½ pound (225 g) ground dark turkey meat (85/15)

¼ cup (10 g) chopped fresh herbs, such as parsley, sage, tarragon, chives, or a mixture

1 teaspoon Quatre Épices (page 80)

¾ teaspoon herbes de Provence or dried thyme

2½ teaspoons kosher salt

½ teaspoon ground black pepper

2 large eggs, lightly beaten

¼ cup (30 g) pistachios, toasted and coarsely chopped

Boiling water, for the bain marie

Special equipment needed: 1½-quart (1.4-L) terrine or a 10 x 4-inch (25 x 10-cm) loaf pan. Also, you will need a baking dish with sides at least 2 inches (5 cm) high for the bain-marie (water bath).

Arrange an oven rack in the lower third of the oven and preheat the oven to 350°F (175°C). Butter a 6-cup (1.4-L) terrine or loaf pan and line it with a sheet of parchment paper with an overhang of 2 to 3 inches (5 cm to 7.5 cm) on the long sides.

In a medium skillet, melt the 3 tablespoons butter over medium-low heat. Add the onions and cook until soft and translucent, taking care not to let the onions brown, 8 to 10 minutes. Remove from the heat and stir in the Cognac. Set aside and let cool. Put the panko in a small bowl and pour the cream over it; let stand for 5 minutes.

In a large bowl, combine the pork, chicken livers, and turkey. Add the cooled onion mixture, the soaked panko, fresh herbs, Quatre Épices, herbes de Provence, salt, pepper, eggs, and pistachios. Use your hands to mix until well blended and a handful of the mixture holds together. Do not overwork the mixture.

To test the seasoning level, in a small skillet over medium-high heat, fry a flat, nickel-sized patty of the mixture for 2 minutes on each side. Taste and adjust the seasoning if necessary.

Gently pack the meat mixture into the terrine pan, making sure not to leave any air pockets. Press down evenly, forming a slightly mounded top. Fold the parchment paper overhang up to cover the mixture. Place a lid on the terrine if you have one, then wrap the entire terrine with aluminum foil and seal tightly.

Place the terrine in a baking dish with sides at least 2 inches (5 cm) high and pour boiling water into the baking dish to come about halfway up the sides of the terrine.

COOKING TIPS

The test for tasting the seasoning in the terrine also works wonderfully for any ground meat recipes such as meatballs, burgers, and meat loaf.

MAKE IT BEAUTIFUL To showcase this, leave the country pâté in the terrine pan and adorn with fresh herbs—it makes for a lovely visual. Flowering chives and tarragon sprigs are always lovely and very French.

Place the terrine in the oven and cook for 1½ hours. Unwrap and test the terrine with an instant-read thermometer, which should read 160°F (71°C). If not to that temperature, rewrap the terrine, return it to the oven, and check again at 5-minute intervals until done. Remove the terrine from the water, unwrap, and let cool completely at room temperature.

Loosely cover the terrine with aluminum foil and place a heavy can, a foil-wrapped brick, or a heavy pot on top of the terrine and refrigerate overnight. Note: This step is almost as important as the actual baking because it compacts the terrine and gives it its classic shape.

To unmold the terrine, run an offset spatula around the edges of the terrine to loosen it. Invert the terrine mold onto a work surface, top with a small cutting board or sheet pan, and invert it again. Remove and discard the parchment paper. Cut the terrine into ½-inch (12-mm) slices and serve.

MARTINI O'CLOCK

My friend April from San Diego—who loves martinis, pineapple, and Hawaii— was the inspiration for this menu. When she came to visit me in San Francisco, we went to a luxurious rooftop lounge bar that served a few varieties of martini flights. We adored going there. This menu uses pineapple in both the cheese balls and the martini. The sweet, fruity flavor of pineapple complements the delicate taste of the "krab" salad canapés. This swanky menu is spectacular served for a NYE cocktail party. **Serves 4 to 6**

Pineapple–Jalapeño Cheese Balls (page 86)
Pineapple–Lime Martini (page 86)
Krab with a K Salad (page 87)

ACCOMPANIMENTS
Cucumber medallions, endive leaves, and celery leaves
Sturdy whole-wheat crackers
Blue cheese–stuffed olives
Assorted candied nuts
Candied pretzel medley

TO DRINK
Pineapple Lime Martinis, classic martinis

PUTTING IT TOGETHER
This petite board is simple and sophisticated, highlighting the luscious flavors of the food and drink. Arrange the krab salad canapés on a board along with the cucumber medallions, endive leaves, and celery leaves. Any leftover krab salad can be piled into a bowl and served alongside for easy dipping. Place the cheese balls on a separate small board, surrounded by the crackers. Use small bowls for the olives, nuts, and pretzels, and set out a small glass or jar filled with fancy miniature skewers to spear the olives. Place pretty appetizer plates nearby. Use cocktail picks to artfully display the garnishes for the drinks.

Pineapple–Jalapeño Cheese Balls

A hint of heat from the jalapeño, sweetness from the pineapple, and a coating of pistachio nuts—these miniature cheese balls are irresistible. If you can't find jalapeño cream cheese, add 1 tablespoon finely chopped pickled jalapeños to plain cream cheese.

Makes 12 cheese balls | Serves 4

½ cup (115 g) jalapeño cream cheese, at room temperature

½ cup (75 g) shredded mild Cheddar

½ cup (122 g) canned pineapple tidbits, drained and patted dry

1 tablespoon finely snipped fresh chives

¼ teaspoon garlic salt

Freshly ground black pepper

½ cup (85 g) plus 1 tablespoon salted, roasted pistachios, finely chopped

In a medium bowl, combine the cheeses, pineapple, chives, garlic salt, and pepper to taste and mix with a rubber spatula until blended. Wrap the bowl in plastic wrap and refrigerate for at least 1 hour or as long as overnight.

To assemble, just before serving, spread the pistachios on a small sheet pan. Use a small ice cream scoop to portion the cheese into 1-inch (2.5-cm) balls (about 1 tablespoon) and roll them on the pistachios to coat evenly. Serve at once.

Pineapple–Lime Martini

A frothy, tropical spin on a classic libation, this martini uses pineapple juice, simple syrup, and Rose's Lime Juice. For a crowd, make a pitcher and prep the glasses ahead of time, then pour and garnish when serving.

Makes 2 drinks

Lime Sugar

Grated zest of 2 limes

⅓ cup (65 g) sugar

1 lime wedge

6 fl. ounces (180 ml) vodka

5 fl. ounces (150 ml) unsweetened pineapple juice

¼ cup (60 ml) simple syrup

1½ fl. ounces (45 ml) Rose's Lime Juice

2 fresh pineapple wedges or lime wheels, for garnish

To make the lime sugar, on a small plate, rub the lime zest and sugar together with your fingertips until the oils are released and fragrant.

Rub the rim of each martini glass with the lime wedge. Dip the glasses into the lime sugar to coat the rims, gently pressing into the sugar.

Pour the vodka, pineapple juice, syrup, and Rose's Lime Juice into an ice-filled cocktail shaker and shake vigorously for 30 seconds. Strain into the prepared glasses and garnish each with a pineapple wedge or lime wheel.

Krab with a K Salad

This recipe uses krab, an imitation crabmeat made from white fish, to make a budget-friendly but delicious appetizer. Celery slices, leaves, and salt add crunch and a fresh, herby flavor to the krab. For a more sumptuous and decadent salad, substitute the same amount of Dungeness crab. Either way, it is spectacular.

Makes a heaping 2 cups (400 g) | Serves 4

1½ cups (235 g) krab (artificial crabmeat), flake style

¼ cup (25 g) thinly sliced celery

1 tablespoon finely diced shallots

3 tablespoons finely chopped fresh dill, plus more for garnish (optional)

1 handful celery leaves, finely chopped, plus whole leaves for garnish (optional)

1 tablespoon finely chopped fresh flat-leaf parsley

Grated lemon zest from 1 large lemon

1 teaspoon fresh lemon juice

1 tablespoon capers, drained, rinsed, and patted dry

½ cup (120 ml) mayonnaise

1 teaspoon grainy or smooth Dijon Mustard

¼ teaspoon Old Bay Seasoning

Freshly ground black pepper

A pinch of celery salt, if needed

Celery leaves, for garnish

Crackers, celery stalks, cucumber rounds, and/or endive leaves, for serving

In a medium bowl, using your hands, tear and shred the krab apart, then add the celery, shallots, the 3 tablespoons dill, chopped celery leaves, parsley, lemon zest and juice, and capers and stir to combine.

In a small bowl, whisk the mayonnaise, mustard, Old Bay Seasoning, and pepper to taste until blended. Pour the mayonnaise mixture over the krab mixture and dress it well. Taste for salt and add celery salt if needed. Cover and refrigerate for 1 hour before serving.

Garnish the salad with celery leaves. Serve with crackers, celery stalks, cucumber rounds, and/or endive leaves.

MAKE IT BEAUTIFUL To serve individual canapés, top a cracker with about 1 tablespoonful of krab salad and garnish with a celery leaf, a dill sprig, and/or a few capers.

A SIXTIES COCKTAIL PARTY

My parents entertained a lot when I was growing up—they hosted game nights, holiday soirées, and outdoor barbecues. The party fare here re-creates one of their sixties cocktail parties that I really wanted to be included in. When sent to bed early prior to the guests arriving, I was dispirited. I couldn't wait to be old enough to drink elegant cocktails, eat finger foods from a chafing dish, and wear my hair in a beehive. This is a chance for you and your guests to wear party clothes, decorate the room with lighted taper candles, and dance to sixties music. Cheese dip, deviled eggs, and gimlets will put the crowd in the party mood. This would also be a spectacular Halloween party theme. **Serves 4 to 6**

Green Chile Pimento Cheese Dip (page 90)
Curried Deviled Eggs (page 91)
Basil Gimlets (page 93)

ACCOMPANIMENTS
Buttery crackers, such as Ritz
Crudités, including celery sticks with leaves, mini sweet
  rainbow peppers, and radishes
Prepared shrimp cocktail
Lemon slices
Purchased Swedish cocktail meatballs
Fancy cocktail almonds
Flaky salt

TO DRINK
Basil Gimlet

PUTTING IT TOGETHER
A vintage deviled-egg dish is perfect here if you have one, or use a platter if you don't. Garnish the deviled eggs with celery leaves and flaky salt for a dramatic flair. Serve the pimento cheese dip in a small bowl centered on a platter and surrounded with the crackers and the crudités. Arrange the poached shrimp from the shrimp cocktail and lemon slices on another small platter and put the cocktail sauce in a small bowl; garnish with fresh parsley. The meatballs should go in a shallow dish with stylish skewers for serving. Place the almonds in a separate dish with herbs to garnish.

Green Chile Pimento Cheese Dip

Pepper jack cheese and Hatch green chiles from New Mexico spice up this dip to serve with buttery crackers and/or crudités. Hatch green chiles from Hatch, New Mexico, are famous in the culinary world. They are known for their exceptional flavor, and roasting them brings out their smoky, spicy, and earthy notes. This is the most revered crop in New Mexico. Look for fresh Hatch chiles at the end of summer to early fall. The canned versions are available in most supermarkets at different heat levels, from mild to hot.

Makes about 1¾ cups (420 g) | Serves 4

2 cups (230 g) shredded pepper jack cheese

½ cup (115 g) cream cheese, at room temperature (not whipped)

¼ cup (55 g) jarred chopped pimientos, drained and dried with a paper towel

One 4-ounce (55 g) can diced hot or mild Hatch green chiles, drained and patted dry (about ¼ cup)

1 tablespoon mayonnaise

¼ teaspoon garlic salt

¼ teaspoon garlic powder

⅛ teaspoon pimenton (smoked paprika), plus more for sprinkling (optional)

Buttery crackers, such as Ritz, and/or crudités

In a food processor or blender, pulse the cheeses, pimientos, chile, mayonnaise, garlic salt, garlic powder, and the ⅛ teaspoon pimenton until the pimientos and chiles are finely chopped but still visible. Spoon into a bowl and finish with a sprinkle of pimenton, if desired. Use immediately, or cover with plastic wrap and refrigerate for up to 2 weeks. Remove from the refrigerator 15 minutes before serving.

Serve with buttery crackers, such as Ritz, or crudités of choice.

MAKE IT BEAUTIFUL Reserve a few diced pimientos and green chiles to add to the dip just before serving. Studding them throughout the dip adds a little more color and texture.

Curried Deviled Eggs

This variation on traditional paprika-dusted deviled eggs is in homage to my mother, who served that classic dish at many family gatherings. Ground turmeric gives these updated deviled eggs a bright yellow hue, while hot madras curry powder makes them ever so flavorful.

Makes 8 deviled eggs | Serves 4

4 large eggs, hard boiled (see page 64), cooled and sliced in half

3 tablespoons mayonnaise

1 tablespoon finely chopped fresh flat-leaf parsley

1 tablespoon finely chopped fresh chives, plus more for garnish (optional)

1 tablespoon finely chopped celery, plus leaves for garnish (optional)

1 teaspoon yellow mustard

¼ teaspoon ground turmeric

¼ teaspoon hot Madras curry powder, or your favorite curry powder

⅛ teaspoon celery salt

Dash of hot sauce (optional)

Freshly ground black pepper

Flaky salt, for sprinkling (optional)

Cut the cooked eggs in half lengthwise and scoop out the yolks; set the egg white halves aside on a platter or plate.

Transfer the yolks to a small food processor and add the mayonnaise, parsley, the 1 tablespoon chopped chives, chopped celery, mustard, turmeric, curry powder, celery salt, and hot sauce, if using. Blend until very smooth and creamy. Add pepper to taste.

Fit a pastry bag with a medium open-star pastry tip (I use the 1M tip), fill the bag with the yolk filling, and pipe into the egg cavities. You can also fill the eggs using a small spoon or a plastic bag with one corner cut off. Garnish with the chives and/or celery leaves and sprinkle with flaky salt, if using. Serve right away.

RECIPE TIPS

If you are piping the filling, be sure to first process it as smoothly as possible to keep it from clogging the pastry tip. The unfilled eggs can be prepared up to 2 days in advance. Store the egg white halves wrapped in plastic and the filling stored separately in a sealed container.

Basil Gimlet

Gin gimlets are one of my favorite cocktails. It is one of the first "grown-up" beverages that I had with a friend at a sophisticated bar after I had just turned twenty-one. We were going to the opera and I felt so chic drinking a gimlet. This version adds homemade basil syrup, which gives the cocktail a vibrant green color and the fresh taste of basil. Basil sprigs are the perfect garnish here.

Makes 2 drinks

Basil Syrup

½ cup (100 g) sugar

½ cup (120 ml) water

2½ cups (100 g) rinsed fresh basil
  leaves, packed

-≺≺≺-

4 fl. ounces (120 ml) gin

1 fl. ounce (30 ml) Rose's Lime Juice
  or fresh lime juice

3 fl. ounces (90 ml) Basil Syrup
  (above)

Fresh basil sprigs and/or lime wheels,
  for garnish (optional)

For the syrup: In a small saucepan, combine the sugar and water and stir on low heat until the sugar is completely dissolved, about 1 minute. Add the basil leaves and simmer for 5 minutes, swirling the pan occasionally and pressing down on them with the back of a wooden spoon. The leaves will darken while simmering, but that's okay.

Remove the pan from the heat and let the syrup cool to room temperature, about 30 minutes. Using a small sieve set over a jar, drain the syrup and discard the basil. Seal the jar tightly and refrigerate for at least 1 hour or up to 1 week.

Add the gin, lime juice, and basil syrup to a cocktail shaker with ice. Shake vigorously to chill, about 30 seconds. Strain the gimlets into chilled Champagne coupes. If desired, garnish with a basil sprig and/or a lime wheel.

TIP FOR STORING BASIL

Trim the stems of a bunch of basil and stand it in a glass or jar of water on your counter with a plastic bag draped loosely over it. Do not store it in the refrigerator, where the leaves will darken.

MAKE IT BEAUTIFUL Use the freshest, most verdant basil leaves that you can find to make this eye-popping libation all the more captivating. Clip on with a tiny clothespin or place on the top of the gimlet. To add a bit of glamour, decorate with a vase of miniature basil.

MARGARITA MIXER

This menu is a celebration of Mexican food and is based on one of my mom's favorite foods: shrimp. Shrimp ceviche is one of the stars of this menu and freshly fried tostadas are perfect for scooping up each tangy, succulent bite. The mushroom and poblano quesadillas are another family favorite. Both dishes meet their perfect match paired with the Strawberry-Hibiscus Margaritas (page 99). The varied colors in this menu make for a beautiful and festive board. **Serves 4 to 6**

Shrimp Ceviche with Tostadas (page 96)
Mushroom & Poblano Quesadillas (page 98)
Strawberry-Hibiscus Margaritas (page 99)

ACCOMPANIMENTS

Lime wedges, chile-limón seasoning, and fresh cilantro (sprigs and chopped)

Edible flowers, such as micro-marigolds and snapdragon blooms (optional)

Mini tostadas and/or tortilla chips

Whole radishes with their greens

Sliced avocado

Quick & Easy Salsa (page 54)

Guacamole

Mexican crema or sour cream

Pickled jalapeños

Spicy roasted chickpeas

Frozen mini tacos, warmed

Fresh strawberries

TO DRINK
Strawberry Hibiscus Margarita

PUTTING IT TOGETHER
In a wide, shallow serving bowl or on a small deep platter, mound the ceviche. Garnish with lime wedges, a drizzle of olive oil, a dusting of chile-limón seasoning, edible flowers, and cilantro. On a board, arrange the tostadas or tortilla chips, more lime wedges, radishes, avocado slices, and bowls of the Quick & Easy Salsa, guacamole, crema, pickled jalapeños, and chickpeas. Arrange the quesadillas and mini tacos on a parchment-lined tray. Tuck in a few cilantro sprigs in between the quesadillas and mini tacos. Serve the margaritas in your prettiest margarita glasses with the lime sugar and a small bowl of fresh strawberries.

Shrimp Ceviche with Tostadas

Ceviche is refreshing and easy to make, and shrimp ceviche is colorful as well as delicious. I like mine dressed up with cilantro, avocado, a pinch of chile-limón seasoning, a drizzle of olive oil, and a squeeze of lime.

Serves 4

1 pound (455 g) raw large shrimp, peeled, deveined, tails removed, cut into ½-inch (12-mm) pieces

½ cup (120 ml) fresh lime juice (about 5 limes)

¼ cup (35 g) finely diced shallots

¾ cup (105 g) multicolored cherry tomatoes, halved

2/3 cup (100 g) seeded and finely diced English cucumber

¼ cup (10 g) finely chopped fresh cilantro, plus more for garnish (optional)

1 avocado, pitted, peeled, and diced

1 serrano chile, seeded and finely diced

Garlic salt

Chile limón seasoning

Mini tostadas or tortilla chips, for serving

In a medium bowl, combine the shrimp, lime juice, and shallots. Stir to mix. Cover and refrigerate until the shrimp turn opaque, about 30 minutes.

In a separate bowl, combine the tomatoes, cucumber, the ¼ cup (10 g) cilantro, the diced avocado, and the serrano chile. Add the marinated shrimp and its juice and season with the garlic salt and chile-limón seasoning to taste. Serve in a wide shallow bowl or on a small, deep platter. Serve with the tostadas for scooping up the ceviche.

MAKE IT BEAUTIFUL When serving, drizzle the ceviche with olive oil, sprinkle with additional chile-limón seasoning, and garnish with edible flowers, chopped fresh cilantro (sprigs are pretty too), and a few lime wedges.

Mushroom & Poblano Quesadillas

Quesadillas are one of the easiest things to make, and they lend themselves to endless variations. This recipe uses street-size flour tortillas, which are 5 inches (12 cm) in diameter. If you don't have mini tortillas, use a 5-inch (12-cm) round cookie cutter to cut them out of regular flour tortillas. The pairing of smoky poblano chiles with earthy mushrooms is fabulous, and the quesadillas can be assembled ahead of time and cooked just before serving.

Makes 8 quesadillas | Serves 4

Filling

2 poblano chiles

2 teaspoons olive oil

1 tablespoon unsalted butter

1 tablespoon avocado or canola oil

6 ounces (170 g) cremini mushrooms, thinly sliced

½ cup (75 g) fresh or thawed frozen yellow corn kernels

1 clove garlic, minced

½ teaspoon dried oregano, crumbled

Garlic salt

1 cup (115 g) shredded pepper Jack or mild Cheddar cheese

8 mini flour tortillas

1 tablespoon unsalted butter, melted

1 tablespoon avocado or canola oil, plus more as needed

Garnishes

Chopped fresh cilantro, Mexican crema, salsa, diced avocado, and lime wedges

Preheat the oven to 425°F (220°C).

To make the filling, place the chiles on a small sheet pan and brush them on both sides with the olive oil. Roast the chiles for 20 minutes, flipping them over halfway through. Transfer the chiles to a brown paper bag; close the bag and let the chiles cool for 30 minutes.

Wearing rubber gloves, remove the stems, skins, and seeds from the chiles and discard. Finely chop the chiles and set aside.

In a 10-inch (25-cm) nonstick skillet, melt the butter with the avocado oil over medium heat. Add the mushrooms and cook until softened and lightly browned, 4 to 5 minutes. Add the chopped chiles and corn kernels and cook for 2 more minutes. If needed, add a little more oil, then add the garlic and cook for 1 minute. Remove the pan from the heat and spoon the mixture into a small bowl, reserving the skillet. Add the oregano and garlic salt to taste to the filling and let cool to room temperature, about 30 minutes. This step can be done ahead and the mixture stored in the refrigerator before assembling the quesadillas.

To assemble the quesadillas, divide the cheese evenly among the tortillas and place about 1 tablespoon of the filling on each one. Fold them over to close and then brush the melted butter on both sides of the tortillas. In the reserved skillet, heat the 1 tablespoon of avocado oil over medium heat and cook the quesadillas in batches of 4 at a time until golden, 3 to 4 minutes on each side. A little char on the quesadillas makes for a flavorful bite. Use more oil if needed. Using a metal spatula, transfer the quesadillas to a platter. Serve with the garnishes.

MAKE IT BEAUTIFUL I like a little char on these to give them a rustic, homemade quality.

Strawberry–Hibiscus Margarita

This frozen, berrylicious margarita is flavored with homemade hibiscus syrup, Rose's Lime Juice, and elderflower liqueur. The lime sugar on the rim is the perfect finish. If you can find hibiscus flowers, use them to garnish this glamorous take on the classic fruity libation. You can find dried hibiscus petals at specialty markets or online.

Makes 1 drink

Hibiscus Syrup

1 cup (250 ml) water

1 cup (200 g) sugar

⅓ cup (10 g) dried hibiscus petals

1 lime wedge

Lime Sugar (page 86)

1 generous cup (150 g) frozen strawberries

1½ fl. ounces (45 ml) 100 percent agave tequila blanco

¾ fl. ounce (20 ml) Hibiscus Syrup (above)

⅓ fl. ounce (10 ml) Rose's Lime Juice

½ fl. ounce (15 ml) St-Germain elderflower liqueur

1 handful crushed ice or a few large ice cubes

Fresh hibiscus flowers (see Make It Beautiful), strawberries, or lime wheels, for garnish

MAKE IT BEAUTIFUL If you happen to have a hibiscus plant, the flowers are gorgeous in this drink; other- wise, attach a slit strawberry or a lime wheel to the rim of the glass. Hibiscus flowers are found in some floral shops; they can be grown in certain climates and some nurseries also cultivate them for sale. They are native to tropical regions and thrive in warmer climates.

For the hibiscus syrup, in a medium saucepan, combine the water and sugar and bring to a simmer over medium heat until the sugar has completely dissolved. Add the dried hibiscus petals. Bring to a boil, then reduce to a simmer, and cook for 5 minutes. Using a small fine-mesh sieve set over a glass jar, drain the mixture, discarding the solids. Let the liquid cool to room temperature. Use immediately, or seal tightly and refrigerate for up to 1 week.

Rub the rim of a margarita glass with the lime wedge. Put the lime sugar on a small plate and press the glass into the sugar so it coats the rim.

In a high-speed blender, combine the strawberries, tequila, hibiscus syrup, Rose's Lime Juice, elderflower liqueur, and ice and blend on high speed for 1 minute. Pour into the prepared margarita glass and garnish with a hibiscus flower, strawberry, or lime wheel.

ANYTIME SNACKS

Snacks make perfect boards to assemble at the last minute or on a whim. Here you'll find a crudité spread with two homemade dips, a crunchy make-your-own crostini board, and the ultimate cheese board. A beautiful assortment of dim sum delights, an abundant antipasti platter, and chaat-cuterie (a South Asian board) are also excellent options when you need some snacking pleasure. Enjoy!

CRUDITÉS, DIPS & SIPS

Here, two yummy dips, one cold and one warm, are paired with crudités—raw seasonal vegetables like carrots, romanesco florets, radishes, and snap peas. This board is a fun and healthy way to lunch, snack, or segue into dinner. It's an ideal board to put together on farmers' market days when your vegetables are at their peak of flavor and freshness. I love serving these with an array of toasted breads and crackers, such as Italian croccantini, which means "little bite" in Italian.
Serves 4 to 6

Green Chile, Spinach & Artichoke Dip (page 104)
Lemony Dilly Dip (page 105)

ACCOMPANIMENTS
An additional dip of your choice (optional)

Seasonal vegetables, such as romanesco florets, sliced watermelon radishes, peeled tiny carrots, halved sugar snap peas, thinly sliced fennel, and radicchio leaves

Toasted slices of seeded baguette or Crostini (page 108)

Croccantini crackers

TO DRINK
Sauvignon blanc, pinot grigio, or rosé

PUTTING IT TOGETHER
Try to source seasonal vegetables of all different colors. Place the artichoke and dilly dips with serving spreaders on the board with the vegetables. Add another dip or two on the board or on a separate bowl with the crackers and the baguette slices. Place a stack of appetizer plates nearby and arrange all of it on a colorful linen to add flourish.

Green Chile, Spinach & Artichoke Dip

This dreamy, warm dip is perfect for holiday entertaining and is a great make-ahead dish. Rich with spinach, artichoke hearts, mascarpone, and crème fraîche, it's both colorful and satisfying. Hatch green chiles give the dip a spicy Southwestern flavor.

Makes 2²/₃ cups (645 ml) | Serves 4

8 cups (5 ounces/140 g) packed baby spinach

½ cup (115 g) mascarpone or cream cheese, at room temperature

⅓ cup (75 ml) crème fraîche

¼ cup (55 g) canned diced Hatch green chiles, drained

2 tablespoons mayonnaise

1½ cups (185 g) shredded low-moisture mozzarella

One 6½-ounce (185-g) jar marinated artichoke hearts, drained, rinsed, and finely chopped

¼ teaspoon garlic salt

Freshly ground black pepper

Crostini (page 108), crackers, and/or baguette slices, for serving

Preheat the oven to 375°F (190°C). Grease a 2¼ cup (540-ml) oval baking dish with oil.

In a medium frying pan over medium-high heat, cook the spinach with 2 tablespoons of water, using tongs to flip and toss the spinach until wilted, 1 to 2 minutes. Drain in a colander and let cool. Transfer the spinach to a clean muslin dish towel and twist the towel to squeeze out as much moisture from the spinach as possible. Using a large chef's knife, chop the spinach finely.

Put the chopped spinach in a medium bowl and add the mascarpone, crème fraîche, chiles, and mayonnaise and stir to combine. Add ¾ cup (90 g) of the mozzarella and all the artichoke hearts and season with garlic salt and pepper to taste. Using a rubber spatula, mix until blended. Taste and adjust the seasoning. Spoon into the prepared baking dish and sprinkle with the remaining ¾ cup (90 g) mozzarella. (If making this in advance, cover and refrigerate for at least 1 hour or up to overnight.)

Cover the dish with aluminum foil and bake for 10 minutes. Remove the foil and bake until golden and bubbly, 10 more minutes. If desired, place under the broiler, about 5 inches (12 cm) from the heat source, until golden brown, about 1 minute.

Serve hot, with crostini, crackers, and/or baguette slices.

RECIPE TIPS
This recipe can easily be doubled and baked in an 11 x 9-inch (28 x 23-cm) baking dish for a larger crowd. It can be made ahead up until baking and is ideal for transport. Wrap tightly until ready, and then bake just before serving.

MAKE IT BEAUTIFUL You can also use your blow torch on this for a bit of browned and bubbly goodness in lieu of the broiler.

Lemony Dilly Dip

Lemon and dill are a beautiful pair and one of my favorite flavor combinations. Mixed with mascarpone and crème fraîche, they make a lovely cold dip that's a breeze to throw together.

Makes ¾ cup (180 ml) | Serves 4

¼ cup (55 g) mascarpone, at room temperature

¼ cup (60 ml) crème fraîche

¼ cup (10 g) finely chopped fresh dill, plus more for garnish (optional)

1 dill pickle, finely chopped and patted dry with a paper towel

Grated zest of ½ lemon

¼ teaspoon fresh lemon juice

¼ teaspoon garlic salt

¼ teaspoon garlic powder

Freshly ground black pepper

In a small bowl, combine the mascarpone, crème fraîche, the ¼ cup (10 g) chopped dill, and dill pickle. Stir together to blend, then stir in the lemon zest and juice, garlic salt and powder, and black pepper to taste. Serve at once, garnished with dill, if using, or cover and refrigerate the ungarnished dip for up to 1 day.

MAKE IT BEAUTIFUL *Always have extra components such as pickles and herbs to add to your finished dip. If making this ahead, give it another stir to incorporate in case it separates in the refrigerator overnight. Sprinkle with chopped fresh dill just before serving.*

MAKE-YOUR-OWN CROSTINI BOARD

A crostini board allows guests to make their own appetizers and is fun for everybody. This one has two homemade toppings—sautéed mushrooms and herbed ricotta— plus a wealth of toppings that your guests can happily choose from to make their own creative little toasts. **Serves 4 to 6**

Crostini (page 108)
Whipped Herbed Ricotta (page 108)
Garlicky Shiitake Mushrooms (page 109)

ACCOMPANIMENTS
Fresh goat cheese
2 balls burrata, drizzled with extra-virgin olive oil
Fresh blackberries, strawberries, or other berries
Green olive tapenade
Honey
Chopped fresh chives and flat-leaf parsley
Fresh herb sprigs, such as mint, chives, dill, and parsley

TO DRINK
Rosé or cava

PUTTING IT TOGETHER
Lay the crostini out on a medium wooden board. On a separate platter, place the whipped herbed ricotta alongside the goat cheese, adding a small cheese spreader. Pile the garlicky shiitakes alongside and top with plenty of fresh chives and fresh parsley. Tear the balls of burrata in half and place them on a small plate with a drizzle of olive oil. Put the blackberries in a small bowl and the mint sprigs in a small jar of water to keep them fresh. Serve the tapenade in a small bowl garnished with herbs and lemon zest. Add a few spoons and knives for building the crostini. Add a small bowl of honey with a honey dipper.

Crostini

These little toasts of thin-sliced baguette are an elegant base for almost any topping, and they couldn't be easier to make. Cut the baguette slices on an extreme diagonal for long, elegant crostini.

Makes about 40 crostini | Serves 6

1 baguette

¼ cup (60 ml) plus 2 tablespoons
  extra-virgin olive oil

Arrange an oven rack in the center of the oven and preheat the oven to 375°F (190°C).

Cut the baguette into ¼-inch- (6-mm-) thick slices and brush both sides of the bread with the olive oil. Arrange on a sheet pan. Bake until lightly golden brown, 10 to 12 minutes. Transfer each toast to a wire rack to cool completely. Serve immediately, or store in a well-sealed container for up to 24 hours.

BAKING TIP
To freshen stored crostini, place them on a sheet pan in a single layer for about 5 minutes in a preheated 350°F (175°C) oven.

VARIATION
To make bruschetta, use slices from a long bâtard-shaped bread, and bake in a 425°F (220°C) oven until golden and toasted.

Whipped Herbed Ricotta

Milky, mild ricotta makes a smooth, flavorful spread when whipped with fresh herbs. Use any combination of herbs and other seasonings for your own spin. Unless I'm using Bellwether Farms ricotta, which comes in a little basket, I like to drain my ricotta overnight in a fine-mesh sieve lined with a double layer of damp cheesecloth and placed over a bowl.

Makes 1 cup (245 g) | Serves 4

1 cup (245 g) whole-milk ricotta
  cheese, drained (page 119)

Garlic salt or kosher salt and freshly
  ground black pepper

1 tablespoon minced fresh herbs, such
  as chives, thyme, and/or dill

Herb sprigs for garnishing (optional)

Transfer the ricotta to a food processor or blender. Season with the garlic salt and pepper to taste, then add the minced herbs. Process until creamy, about 1 minute. Taste and adjust the seasoning. Serve in a bowl, garnished with herb sprigs, if using.

Garlicky Shiitake Mushrooms

Mushrooms cooked in butter and oil with garlic are a savory and satisfying way to dress up Crostini (opposite). Feel free to swap out the shiitake mushrooms for other types of mushrooms, like chanterelles or cremini.

Serves 4

2 tablespoons unsalted butter

2 tablespoons olive oil

5 ounces (140 g) shiitake mushrooms, washed, dried, and stems trimmed, sliced and/or whole for variety

1 tablespoon fresh thyme leaves

2 cloves garlic, minced

¼ teaspoon garlic salt

Freshly ground black pepper

1 tablespoon finely chopped fresh chives, plus more for garnish

In a medium nonstick skillet, melt the butter over medium heat and add the olive oil. Add the mushrooms and thyme and cook, stirring until the mushrooms release their liquid and become golden, 4 to 5 minutes. Stir in the garlic and garlic salt. Add pepper to taste and the 1 tablespoon chives, stirring gently to blend.

Serve warm in a ramekin, sprinkled with chives.

DIM SUM CELEBRATION

This festive menu of sweet and savory bites—homemade char siu puffs, purchased dumplings, and homemade sesame-almond shortbread—is lovely to serve for Lunar New Year or any time of year. It was created by Christine Gallary, a Chinese-American food editor and prolific recipe developer for the Kitchn website. Christine refers to this board as a "tray of togetherness." It can be served for lunch or a late-afternoon feast. **Serves 4 to 6**

Char Siu Chicken Puffs (page 112)
Dumpling Dipping Sauce (page 112)
Sesame–Almond Shortbread (page 115)

ACCOMPANIMENTS
Cooked frozen dumplings, pot stickers, or gyoza
Shrimp chips and rice crackers
Roasted and salted pistachios
Clementine segments or whole with their leaves and sliced Asian pears

TO DRINK
Jasmine tea or chrysanthemum tea

PUTTING IT TOGETHER
On a large wooden board, arrange the char siu puffs, shortbread, shrimp chips, rice crackers, pistachios, clementines, and Asian pears. Garnish with any citrus leaves. On a separate plate or platter add the other cooked dumplings. Serve the dipping sauce nearby in a small dish. For your Lunar New Year board, add pops of red which signifies good fortune, vitality, celebration, and prosperity and be sure to use six or eight components. The numbers six and eight are lucky in Chinese culture.

Char Siu Chicken Puffs

This recipe for savory stuffed pastries is easily made using store-bought puff pastry and store-bought char siu BBQ sauce. The moist chicken filling is seasoned with five-spice powder and enrobed in delicate, golden flaky pastry.

Makes 16 puffs | Serves 4 to 6

8 ounces (225 g) boneless, skinless chicken thighs

¼ teaspoon Chinese five-spice powder

1 tablespoon canola oil, plus more if needed

¼ cup (35 g) finely diced yellow onion or shallots

3 tablespoons char siu sauce, preferably Lee Kum Kee

Two 8-ounce (225-g) sheets puff pastry, thawed according to package directions

1 large egg beaten with 1 teaspoon water, for egg wash

Dumpling Dipping Sauce

To make a quick dipping sauce for dumplings, in a bowl, stir together 2 tablespoons rice vinegar, 2 tablespoons soy sauce, 1 teaspoon chile crunch, and some chopped green onion.

Pat the chicken dry with paper towels. Season all over with the five-spice powder. In a small skillet, heat the 1 tablespoon oil over medium heat until it shimmers. Add the chicken and cook until browned and cooked through, 3 to 4 minutes per side. Using tongs, transfer to a cutting board to cool.

Add the onion to the pan, reducing the heat to medium-low and adding more oil if needed. Cook and stir the onion until translucent, about 5 minutes. Remove the pan from the heat and set aside. Finely chop the chicken. Add the chicken and char siu sauce to the onion in the pan and stir to combine. Transfer the chicken mixture to a container, spreading it into an even layer, seal tightly, and refrigerate for at least 30 minutes or up to overnight.

Position two oven racks evenly in the oven and preheat to 400°F (205°C). Line 2 sheet pans with parchment paper.

To assemble the puffs, roll out one sheet of the puff pastry on a lightly floured work surface to a ⅛ (3 mm) thickness. Using a 3½-inch (9-cm) round cutter, cut out as many rounds as you can (7 to 8 from each sheet). Top each round with a scant 1 tablespoonful of filling. Using a pastry brush, coat the edges of the rounds with a very thin layer of the egg wash. Fold the rounds in half and stretch the edges slightly while pressing them together to seal. Using the tines of a fork, crimp the sealed edges to seal completely. Repeat with the second sheet of puff pastry and the remaining filling.

Transfer the pastries to the prepared sheet pans, spacing them evenly apart and placing half on each sheet pan. Give them one more reinforced crimp with a fork and then brush the tops lightly and evenly with the egg wash.

Bake until golden brown all over, 15 to 17 minutes. Let them cool on the pans for at least 5 minutes. Serve warm or at room temperature, or let cool completely and store in an airtight container in the refrigerator for up to 4 days. Reheat in a 325°F (165°C) oven until warmed through, about 8 minutes.

Sesame–Almond Shortbread

These standout cookies are sure to make it to the top of the list for any shortbread aficionado or cookie lover. Their delicate nutty taste and buttery texture make this shortbread exquisite. The sweet glaze adds even more almond flavor, and the black and white sesame seeds add crunch. They have the added virtue of storing well, so you can make them in advance of serving.

Makes 40 to 48 cookies

1 cup (225 g) unsalted butter, at room temperature

½ cup (100 g) granulated sugar

¼ cup (30 g) confectioners' sugar

¾ teaspoon fine sea salt

1 large egg yolk

1¼ teaspoons almond extract

2 cups (250 g) all-purpose flour

Glaze

1 tablespoon black sesame seeds

1 tablespoon white sesame seeds, toasted (see page 28)

1 cup (100 g) confectioners' sugar, sifted

2 tablespoons milk, any fat percentage

½ teaspoon almond extract

Pinch of fine sea salt

In a stand mixer fitted with the paddle attachment, beat the butter on low speed until creamy, 1 to 2 minutes. Add the granulated sugar, confectioners' sugar, and salt. Beat on low speed until just combined, about 1 minute. Using a narrow rubber spatula, scrape down the paddle and the sides of the bowl. Add the egg yolk and almond extract and beat on low speed for 1 minute. Add the flour and beat on low speed until the flour is just blended in and the dough forms a mass around the paddle, about 1 minute.

On a lightly floured surface, divide the dough in half. Shape each half into a smooth ball, then roll into a log about 5½ inches (14 cm) long and 1¾ inches (4.5 cm) thick. Place each log on a 12-inch (30.5-cm) sheet of plastic wrap or parchment paper. Wrap the logs in the plastic, twisting the ends closed, then roll the logs on the counter a few times to tighten the plastic wrap. Refrigerate the logs until firm, at least 2 hours or up to 1 week before baking.

To bake the cookies, line a baking sheet with parchment paper or a Silpat baking mat. Arrange a rack in the center of the oven and preheat the oven to 350°F (175°C).

Unwrap one dough log and place it on a cutting board. Trim the ends of the log, then cut it crosswise into ¼ inch (6 mm) thick rounds to make 20 to 24 rounds. Transfer the rounds to the prepared baking sheet, spacing them ½ inch (12 mm) apart. Bake until lightly golden on the edges, 10 to 14 minutes, rotating the baking sheet from front to back halfway through baking. Let cool for a few minutes on the baking sheet and then transfer the cookies to a wire rack to cool completely. Repeat to slice and bake the second dough log on the same baking sheet.

To make the glaze, stir the sesame seeds together in a small bowl. In another bowl, combine the confectioners' sugar, milk, almond extract, and salt and whisk until smooth. Drizzle the glaze over the cookies in a zigzag pattern. Sprinkle with the sesame seeds. Let stand until the glaze is set, about 20 minutes. Serve now or store in an airtight container at room temperature for up to 4 days.

THE ULTIMATE CHEESE BOARD

Cheese boards, those delightful offerings that make their appearance after the dessert course in France, are also brilliant served before dinner or in place of lunch or supper. This one features a rich green-chile dip along with an herby baked ricotta served with hot honey, plus an array of accompaniments to make this a cheese board of your dreams. The cheeses we used for this board were from Graze + Gather Co.: Valley Ford's "Grazin' Girl"; Capriole's Julianna, an aged goat cheese; and Roelli's Red Rock cheddar. You can easily make this a gluten-free cheese board using gluten-free crackers and breads. This is also very suitable for the vegetarians at your table as it features seasonal veggies and fruit. **Serves 4 to 6**

Green Chile Millionaire Dip (page 118)
Baked Herbed Ricotta with Hot Honey (page 119)

ACCOMPANIMENTS

A variety of colorful cheeses with different textures and flavors, such as a blue cheese like Stilton or Gorgonzola, a flower-and-herb-laced fresh goat cheese, and an aged cheddar

Seasonal crudités such as cucumber spears, mini sweet peppers, thinly sliced radishes, Sungold cherry tomatoes, and zucchini ribbons

Fresh figs and/or grapes, or other seasonal fruits

Dried fruits, such as apricots

Roasted sesame-coated almonds and/or quicos (giant crunchy corn)

Sliced seeded baguette and/or Crostini (page 108)

Crackers, cheese coins, and/or cheese straws

Pickled vegetables, such as curried cauliflower pickles

Olives, such as Castelvetrano

Hot honey, honeycomb, mango chutney, or strawberry-fig jam

Edible flowers, such as squash blossoms and micro-marigolds (optional)

TO DRINK

Pinot grigio, sauvignon blanc, or another floral white wine or rosé

PUTTING IT TOGETHER

This is a showstopper of a feast, so choose the largest board that you have! Think abundance, punchy colors, boldness, and an endless array of deliciousness. Place the Green-Chile Millionaire Dip and the baked ricotta in bowls directly on the board, then arrange the cheeses alongside; include cheese knives for slicing and spreading. Fill in the board with the seasonal crudités and fresh and dried fruits. Scatter the almonds and quicos throughout the board. Arrange the baguette or crostini slices along with the crackers, cheese coins, and/or cheese straws on a plate or another small board. In other little vessels, add the pickled vegetables, olives, extra almonds, hot honey with a dipper, honeycomb, and jam. Decorate with edible flowers if you like; it adds a great pop of color.

Green Chile Millionaire Dip

The Millionaire Dip, so-called for its richness, is also called Neiman Marcus Dip. Developed and created for the original Neiman Marcus restaurant in Texas in the 1950s by Helen Corbitt, a cookbook author and chef, the Neiman Marcus Dip includes bacon and Cheddar cheese. My version uses green chiles and Monterey Jack cheese but is equally delicious—and rich.

Makes 2 cups (480 ml) | Serves 6 to 8

½ cup (85 g) plus 1 tablespoon slivered almonds

One 8-ounce (225-g) package cream cheese, at room temperature

½ cup (120 ml) mayonnaise

2 cups (230 g) shredded Monterey Jack cheese

5 green onions, green and pale green parts only, thinly sliced

One 4-ounce (115-g) can diced Hatch green chiles, drained well

½ teaspoon pimenton (smoked paprika) plus more for garnish

¼ teaspoon garlic salt

¼ teaspoon freshly ground black pepper

Crackers or sliced bread, for serving

Preheat the oven to 350°F (175°C). Spread the almonds on a small baking sheet and toast in the oven, stirring once or twice, until lightly golden, about 7 minutes. Remove from the oven and set aside to cool.

In a medium bowl, combine the cream cheese, mayonnaise, and Monterey Jack cheese. Stir with a rubber spatula until smooth. Fold in 4 of the green onions and all the green chiles. Season with the ½ teaspoon pimenton, garlic salt, and pepper. Fold in all but 1 tablespoon of the almonds.

Spoon the dip into a bowl. Cover and refrigerate for at least 2 hours or up to overnight before serving. Remove from the refrigerator 15 minutes before serving. To serve, sprinkle with the remaining almonds and remaining green onion and dust lightly with a little more pimenton.

Baked Herbed Ricotta with Hot Honey

A warm, creamy baked cheese will elevate your cheese board to the ultimate! Flavored with Italian seasoning and orange zest, it's finished with a drizzle of olive oil, hot honey, and a sprinkle of flaky salt. If you don't have hot honey, simply add a pinch of red pepper flakes to regular honey. Taste the ricotta before salting, depending on the cheese you use, it might not be needed.

Makes 2 cups (480 ml) | Serves 4 to 6

2 cups (448 g) whole-milk ricotta

¼ cup (25 g) plus 2 tablespoons grated Pecorino Romano

1 tablespoon olive oil, plus more for drizzling

1 teaspoon Italian seasoning

Grated zest of 1 orange or lemon

Garlic salt or kosher salt and freshly ground black pepper

Pinch of red pepper flakes (optional)

Hot honey or regular honey, for drizzling

1 fresh rosemary sprig, for garnish

Flaky salt, for sprinkling

Crackers, Crostini (page 108), or baguette slices, for serving

Drain the ricotta: Line a large fine-mesh sieve with two layers of damp cheesecloth and place over a medium bowl. Add the ricotta and fold the ends of the cheesecloth over it. Weigh the cheese down with a heavy bowl. Refrigerate for at least 8 hours or preferably overnight. Discard the drained liquid (whey) or use it in soups or to make bread.

Preheat the oven to 375°F (190°C). Oil a 2¼ cup (540 ml) baking dish.

In a medium bowl, combine the drained ricotta, the ¼ cup (25 g) Pecorino, the 1 tablespoon olive oil, Italian seasoning, orange zest, salt and black pepper to taste, and red pepper flakes, if using. Mix with a rubber spatula until blended. Taste and adjust the seasoning. Scrape into the prepared baking dish and sprinkle with the remaining 2 tablespoons Pecorino.

Place the baking dish on a small sheet pan and bake until slightly golden, about 15 minutes. Place under the broiler about 5 inches (12 cm) from the heat source, and broil until bubbling slightly, 1 to 2 minutes. Let cool on a wire rack for 5 minutes, then drizzle with olive oil and hot honey. Garnish with a rosemary sprig and a sprinkle of flaky salt. Serve warm or at room temperature with crackers, crostini, or baguette slices.

MAKE IT BEAUTIFUL If you have a kitchen blowtorch, use it instead of your broiler to slightly brown and caramelize the top.

CHAAT-CUTERIE BOARD

This menu of South Asian snacks, or chaat, comes from cookbook author, columnist, and food blogger Amisha Gurbani. Her savory vegetarian potato and pea samosas are exceptional, especially when served with her cilantro-mint chutney, which does double duty with the delightful marinated paneer skewers. **Serves 4 to 6**

Potato & Pea Samosas with Cilantro–Mint Chutney (page 123)
Tikka Paneer Cocktail Skewers (page 125)

ACCOMPANIMENTS
Chevda snack mix, and chakri spirals
Masala peanuts
Lemon slices
Cilantro sprigs
Ketchup (optional)

TO DRINK
Masala chai, chaat masala lemonade, Riesling, or light beer

PUTTING IT TOGETHER
Place the samosas on a platter with sprigs of fresh cilantro. On a medium board, arrange the skewers with sprigs of cilantro, along with bowls of the chakri spirals, chevda snack mix, masala peanuts, and lemon slices. Place small bowls of the cilantro–mint chutney and the ketchup alongside the platter and board, and include serving spoons. Have a stack of appetizer plates alongside.

Potato & Pea Samosas with Cilantro–Mint Chutney

Food blogger Amisha Gurbani's mother-in-law taught her this great hack of using store-bought flour tortillas in place of flaky pastry for samosas. It's both tasty and a real time saver when making this classic South Asian appetizer. Note: The filling can be made 1 day ahead, and the samosas can be made 2 to 3 days before frying if kept well sealed. Serve these with Cilantro-Mint Chutney and ketchup as Amisha recommends: "As kids we liked everything with ketchup, so the habit carried on to adulthood."

Makes 18 to 20 samosas | Serves 4 to 6

Filling

2 russet potatoes (650 g total), scrubbed

½ teaspoon fennel seeds

½ teaspoon coriander seeds

4 tablespoons (60 ml) avocado or canola oil, plus more if needed

1 leek, white and pale green parts only, thinly sliced into half-moons

½ cup (65 g) finely diced red onion

1 Thai or 2 serrano chiles, seeded and finely diced

½-inch (12-mm) piece fresh ginger, peeled

1 cup (135 g) fresh or thawed frozen green peas

½ teaspoon Kashmiri chili powder

½ teaspoon garam masala

½ teaspoon amchur powder

¾ teaspoon kosher salt

¾ teaspoon sugar

1 tablespoon fresh lemon juice

⅓ cup (15 g) finely chopped fresh cilantro

To make the filling, in a large pot of salted boiling water, cook the potatoes until firm but knife-tender, 15 to 20 minutes; the potatoes should be a tad firm because you will continue to cook them in the skillet. Drain, let cool, and peel. Cut the potatoes into ¼-inch (6-mm) dice and let them cool completely.

In a small pan on medium heat, toast the fennel and coriander seeds until fragrant, about 3 minutes. Transfer to a spice grinder or mortar and pestle, then grind to a coarse powder and set aside.

In a large nonstick skillet, heat 2 tablespoons of the oil over medium heat. Add the leek and red onion and cook, stirring occasionally, until tender, 4 to 5 minutes.

While the vegetables cook, make a paste with the Thai or serrano chiles and ginger using a mortar and pestle.

When the vegetables have softened, add the reserved fennel-coriander mixture and the chile-ginger paste. Cook, stirring constantly, for 2 more minutes, then transfer to a bowl and set aside.

Add the remaining 2 tablespoons of oil to the pan and add the reserved potatoes. Cook over medium heat, stirring occasionally, until lightly browned, 12 to 15 minutes; add more oil if needed. Reduce the heat to low and add the reserved leek mixture, the green peas, chili powder, garam masala, amchur powder, salt, sugar, and lemon juice. Stir well to combine, then stir in the cilantro. Taste and adjust the seasoning.

Let the filling cool completely. If not using right away, you can refrigerate the filling in an airtight container up to 2 days in advance.

continued...

continued...

Cilantro-Mint Chutney

3 cups (135 g) packed coarsely chopped fresh cilantro

½ cup (25 g) coarsely chopped fresh mint

½ cup (125 ml) water

2 tablespoons fresh lemon juice

2 tablespoons lightly salted roasted peanuts

2 teaspoons organic sugar

2 cloves garlic, smashed

1 serrano chile or 2 Thai green chiles, seeded and chopped

1 teaspoon cumin seeds

1 teaspoon kosher salt

―――

1 tablespoon all-purpose flour

9 or 10 store-bought flour tortillas (6 to 7 inches/15 to 17 cm) in diameter), halved

Avocado oil, for frying

Ketchup, for serving (optional)

To make the chutney, combine all the ingredients in a blender and process to a smooth sauce. Pour the chutney into an 8-ounce (240-ml) glass jar and cover tightly. You can refrigerate the chutney in an airtight container with plastic wrap pressed directly on the surface of the chutney (to prevent oxidization), up to 1 week. If oxidation does occur, just scrape off the top.

To assemble and cook the samosas, line a sheet pan with paper towels and place a wire rack on top. Line a second sheet pan with parchment paper. In a small bowl, combine the flour and 1½ tablespoons water and whisk until blended to make a flour paste for sealing the tortillas.

Keeping the tortillas in the package they come in as you work, lay a tortilla half on a work surface with the curved edge on the right. Pinch the middle of the curved side and fold the bottom edge up to overlap where you are pinching. While continuing to pinch the tortilla, roll the tortilla into a cone shape, making sure that the bottom of the cone (where you are pinching) doesn't have an opening. Dab the flour paste along the top edge of the tortilla and press to seal; it should now look like an ice cream cone. Spoon the potato and pea mixture into the cone. Using your finger or a pastry brush, dab the flour paste on the excess tortilla at the top and fold it over the filling to create a triangle. Transfer to the prepared pan. Repeat to use all the filling and the tortillas.

Add 2 inches (5 cm) oil to a Dutch oven or heavy sauté pan and heat to 350°F (175°C) on a deep-frying thermometer.

Fry the samosas 6 at a time until light golden brown, turning them over with tongs halfway through cooking. Using tongs, transfer them to the wire rack to drain.

Place the samosas on a serving tray and serve hot with the Cilantro-Mint Chutney and ketchup, if using.

COOKING TIPS
Make sure to use the freshest tortillas you can find so they won't crack or break. If they aren't fresh they will be harder to shape.

The samosas can be made ahead before frying. Place in an airtight container, separating the layers with parchment paper, and store in the refrigerator for 2 to 3 days or freeze for up to 1 month (thaw frozen samosas and bring to room temperature before frying). Fry the samosas right before serving.

Tikka Paneer Cocktail Skewers

The tikka marinade for these skewers bursts with the flavor of a host of Indian spices. Tikka means "small chunks of food," and cutting the paneer cheese, bell pepper, and onion into uniform ½-inch (12-mm) pieces can be a fun task for kids or a few friends. The tiny skewers are elegant on the board and tantalizing on the palate. Check the paneer package to see if it needs to be pre-soaked before using.

Makes 12 skewers | Serves 4

6 ounces (170 g) paneer, cut into ½-inch (12-mm) cubes

½ cup (120 ml) plain Greek yogurt

1 tablespoon fresh lemon juice

1½ teaspoons olive oil

2 cloves garlic, grated

½ inch (12 mm) fresh ginger, peeled and grated

¾ teaspoon kosher salt

¼ teaspoon Kashmiri red chili powder

½ teaspoon ground turmeric

½ teaspoon garam masala

½ teaspoon chaat masala

½ teaspoon ground coriander

½ teaspoon ground cumin

¼ teaspoon amchur powder

Twelve 6-inch (15-cm) bamboo skewers

½ red or yellow bell pepper, seeded, deveined, and cut into ½-inch (12-mm) cubes

½ red onion, cut into ½-inch (12-mm) cubes

1 tablespoon avocado or canola oil, for brushing

Lemon wedges, Cilantro-Mint Chutney (page 123), and cilantro sprigs, for serving

Soak the paneer cubes in hot water for 15 minutes to soften the cheese. Drain well and set aside.

In a medium bowl, combine the yogurt, lemon juice, olive oil, garlic, ginger, salt, and all the spices and whisk to combine.

Add the paneer and gently stir with your hands to coat it with the mixture. Cover with plastic wrap and refrigerate for at least 1 hour or as long as overnight.

Preheat the oven to 400°F (205°C). Line 2 small sheet pans with parchment paper. Place the bamboo skewers in warm water to cover for 15 minutes, then drain well.

On a skewer, spear a cube of paneer, bell pepper, and onion in that order, repeating to fill the skewer. Repeat with the remaining skewers.

Place 6 skewers 1 inch (2.5 cm) apart on each prepared sheet pan. Using a pastry brush, brush each skewer with the remaining marinade to coat thoroughly, then brush with the oil.

Place the pans on the bottom rack of the oven and bake until lightly browned, about 20 minutes, rotating the pan halfway through baking. To finish, broil the skewers 5 inches (12 cm) from the heat source for about 1 minute. Transfer the pans to wire racks to let the skewers cool for a few minutes, then serve them immediately, with lemon wedges, chutney, and cilantro.

MAKE IT BEAUTIFUL I love a slight char on these but keep your eye on them so they don't get too dark. Place the skewers on a platter with a bowl of the Cilantro-Mint Chutney in the center and tuck in some lemon wedges and sprigs of cilantro. You can also add chopped cilantro to garnish.

ANTIPASTI PLATTER

Antipasti, a medley of different kinds of offerings, means "before the meal" in Italian, and a plate laden with small bites was one of the original inspirations for food boards, platters, and trays. This menu features two kinds of skewers—tortellini and fruit—along with stuffed mushrooms. We love having an antipasti platter on the weekends before our main meal, and sometimes, this ends up becoming our entire meal. **Serves 4 to 6**

Tortellini Skewers (page 128)
Melon, Grape & Prosciutto Skewers (page 128)
Italian Stuffed Mushrooms (page 129)

ACCOMPANIMENTS

Burrata and a Parmesan wedge

Mortadella

Sliced focaccia, taralli (Italian crackers), and/or Herbes de Provence Grissini (page 60)

Giardiniera (Italian pickled vegetable relish), peperoncinis, marinated artichoke hearts, caperberries

Almonds

Fig jam

Pesto sauce, good-quality balsamic vinegar, and extra-virgin olive oil

Fresh rosemary sprigs, thyme sprigs, and basil leaves, for garnish

TO DRINK

Prosecco or Aperol spritzes

PUTTING IT TOGETHER

On a large wooden board, arrange the burrata and Parmesan wedge along with the mortadella, sliced focaccia, taralli, grissini, and almonds. Add small bowls of the giardiniera, peperoncinis, marinated artichoke hearts, caperberries, and fig jam, both on and off the board. Garnish with herb sprigs. Put the pesto sauce, balsamic vinegar, and olive oil in small bowls and serve alongside. On separate plates or small platters, arrange the stuffed mushrooms and skewers, garnishing with basil leaves. Glasses of bubbling prosecco round out this antipasti feast. For that glamour shot, pour the prosecco right before serving for that effervescent flair.

Tortellini Skewers

Store-bought fresh tortellini skewered with cherry tomatoes, basil leaves, and mozzarella balls are beyond easy to prepare. Served with store-bought pesto and good-quality balsamic vinegar for dipping, these little appetizers are ideal for antipasti platters.

Makes 16 skewers | Serves 4

16 fresh tortellini with any filling

Olive oil, for drizzling

16 cherry tomatoes

16 fresh basil leaves, plus more for garnish

8 ounces (225 g) fresh ciliegine (cherry-sized mozzarella balls)

Sixteen 5-inch (12-cm) miniature skewers or cocktail picks

Store-bought pesto sauce and balsamic vinegar, for serving

Cook the tortellini according to package directions just until al dente; be sure not to overcook. Drain well in a colander or sieve and drizzle them with a little olive oil as they cool to room temperature. For each skewer, spear one tortellini, a tomato, a folded-in-half basil leaf, and a mozzarella ball. Repeat to make 16 skewers.

Place the skewers on a platter with the pesto sauce and balsamic vinegar in little bowls for serving. Garnish with basil leaves, if desired, and drizzle with a little more olive oil.

Melon, Grape & Prosciutto Skewers

This appetizer couldn't be easier! You could also use green grapes and honeydew instead of the cantaloupe and red grapes for these simple but flavorful skewers.

Makes 16 skewers

16 cantaloupe balls

4 thin slices of prosciutto, quartered

16 fresh ciliegine balls (cherry-sized mozzarella balls)

16 red seedless grapes

For each skewer, spear and thread the one cantaloupe ball, a quarter piece of prosciutto, one mozzarella ball, and one grape. Serve.

Italian Stuffed Mushrooms

These spicy stuffed mushrooms are a delectable addition to any antipasti menu. If spicy doesn't work for you, use mild Italian sausage and leave out the red pepper flakes and chile powder. This easy appetizer will still be savory and satisfying.

Makes 16 stuffed mushrooms | Serves 4

16 large cremini or white button mushrooms, washed, dried, and stemmed (reserve stems)

Olive oil, for brushing and drizzling

4 ounces (115 g) hot or mild Italian sausage

½ teaspoon fennel seeds

½ teaspoon red pepper flakes (optional)

½ teaspoon Italian seasoning

¼ teaspoon hot Calabrian chile powder, or double the red pepper flakes

6 fresh basil leaves, finely chopped, plus small leaves for garnish (optional)

1 tablespoon finely chopped fresh flat-leaf parsley, plus more for garnish (optional)

2 cloves garlic, minced

½ cup (50 g) packed finely grated fresh Parmesan, plus more for garnish

4 Castelvetrano olives, pitted and finely chopped

Salt and freshly ground black pepper

Arrange a rack in the center of the oven and preheat to 375°F (190°C). Line a small sheet pan with parchment paper. Place the mushrooms cavity side down on the prepared pan and brush them with olive oil.

To make the filling, finely chop the reserved mushroom stems and place them in a small bowl. In a medium nonstick skillet over medium heat, cook the sausage, stirring occasionally, until no longer pink, about 3 minutes, breaking it up with a wooden spoon. Add the fennel seeds, red pepper flakes (if using), Italian seasoning, and chile powder and stir to combine. Add the chopped basil and the 1 tablespoon parsley and cook for 1 minute. Lower the heat and add the reserved chopped mushroom stems and the garlic, cooking just until fragrant, about 1 minute. Remove from the heat and transfer the filling to a bowl. Let cool for 10 minutes. Add the ½ cup Parmesan and olives. Taste and season with salt and pepper if needed.

Turn the mushrooms over and brush them with olive oil. Using a small spoon, fill the mushroom cavities generously with the filling, pressing it into the cavities. Bake the mushrooms until they sizzle and their juices have rendered, 8 to 10 minutes.

Arrange the stuffed mushrooms on a serving tray and if desired, drizzle with olive oil and sprinkle with a little more Parmesan. Garnish with basil leaves, if using. Serve warm.

COOKING TIPS

Use similarly sized large mushrooms for this recipe. Look for cremini mushrooms in the market; they are about 2 inches (5 cm) in diameter. If you can't find them, use similarly sized white button mushrooms. If you have any filling leftover, it is scrumptious added to scrambled eggs.

SWEETS FOR THE SWEET

If you have never had a chocolate fondue party, what are you waiting for? A cheese, cherry, and chocolate dessert board is lovely in summer or when cherries are in season wherever you reside. A big cookie platter is one of the easiest ways to serve dessert, and all you strawberry fans out there will adore the strawberry feast in this chapter. Our halva board celebrates all things sesame, especially a blondie made with tahini, pistachios, and halva (one of my favorite recipes in this book). These are the perfect endings for any meal.

CHOCOLATE LOVER'S SOIRÉE

If you adore chocolate, this one's for you! Chocolate fondue, chocolate shortbread, and Chocolate Chip Biscotti (page 142) star on this menu, along with an array of toppings and add-ons that will satisfy all your cravings. This makes for a delightful engagement or Valentine's Day party. **Serves 4 to 6**

Milk Chocolate Fondue (page 134)
Chocolate–Cinnamon Shortbread (page 135)

ACCOMPANIMENTS

Berries, such as strawberries and raspberries

Seasonal fruit, such as fresh figs, sliced oranges, apples, pears, or bananas

Biscotti, pretzels, marshmallows, pound cake cubes, and/or Rice Krispie squares

Chocolate bark

Chopped pistachios, cacao nibs, dried cherries, and pomegranate arils

Fresh mint sprigs, such as chocolate mint

TO DRINK

Champagne or sparkling rosé

PUTTING IT TOGETHER

Place your fondue pot and fondue forks on a platter or board and surround it with the berries, seasonal fruit, and mint sprigs. On another board or platter, arrange the shortbread, biscotti, pretzels, marshmallows, pound cake cubes, Rice Krispie squares, and chocolate bark. I like to serve additional frosted shortbread on a separate plate with Chocolate Chip Biscotti (page 142). Add small bowls of chopped pistachios, cacao nibs, dried cherries, and pomegranate arils to sprinkle onto fondue-dipped treats, which adds texture and flavor.

Milk Chocolate Fondue

This creamy chocolate fondue will keep you coming back for more. It's so easy to make using milk chocolate chips and heavy cream. Look for Tahitian vanilla extract to use here; its fruity profile adds nuances of cherry, licorice, and caramel. If you don't have a fondue pot, use a large, 2-cup (480-ml) ramekin set over a candle food warmer, also known as Sterno.

Makes 2 cups (480 ml) | Serves 4

One package (11½ ounces/325 g) milk chocolate chips

¾ cup (180 ml) heavy cream

1½ teaspoons Tahitian or regular vanilla extract

Pinch of kosher salt

Put the chocolate chips in a medium glass bowl. Add the cream to a medium saucepan and gently warm it over low heat until bubbles form around the edges of the pan. Pour the warmed cream over the chocolate chips and let stand for 2 minutes. Using a small rubber spatula, stir until smooth. Stir in the vanilla and salt.

Pour the mixture into a fondue pot and serve with fresh fruits, cookies, and other treats (see page 133). Any leftover fondue will keep, covered, in the refrigerator for up to 1 week. Rewarm over low heat in a double boiler, stirring gently.

Chocolate–Cinnamon Shortbread

This cozy, flavorful shortbread has rich Dutch-process cocoa, warming cinnamon, and a pinch of hot chile powder. It's reminiscent of the Mexican hot chocolate I used to share with my mom when I visited New Mexico and we would go out to lunch. You will need to make the dough a day before baking, as the dough requires an overnight chill in the refrigerator. This is a great cookie for a host or holiday gift. The frosting is optional—leave it off for shortbreads you want to dip in the fondue (opposite) or add it as a special treat with the sprinkles (I often do both!).

Makes 1½ to 2 dozen cookies

½ cup (115 g) salted butter, preferably European style, at room temperature

½ cup (60 g) confectioners' sugar, sifted

1 cup (125 g) all-purpose flour, sifted

¼ cup (25 g) Dutch-process cocoa powder, plus more for rolling (optional)

1 teaspoon ground cinnamon

Pinch of New Mexico chile powder, or your favorite chile powder

Pinch of kosher salt

½ cup (125 ml) chocolate frosting, homemade or store-bought (optional)

Sprinkles, jimmies, or nonpareils, for sprinkling (optional)

MAKE IT BEAUTIFUL Clean any crumbs from your offset spatula while frosting the cookies to keep the frosting crumb-free. These cookies make a wonderful gift and have endless possibilities with all the decorative holiday sprinkles on the market. Also, try different cookie cutter shapes to add personality.

In a stand mixer fitted with a paddle attachment, cream the butter on medium speed until fluffy, about 1 minute total, scraping down the paddle and sides of the bowl with a rubber spatula as needed. Lower the speed and gradually add the confectioners' sugar until thoroughly combined. Scrape down the sides of the bowl and the paddle once more.

In a small bowl, combine the flour, the ¼ cup (25 g) cocoa powder, cinnamon, chile powder, and salt. Stir with a whisk to blend. With the mixer on low, gradually add the flour mixture just until blended; don't overmix. Scrape down the sides and the bottom of the bowl with the rubber spatula if needed. Turn out the dough and press it into a ball, flatten it into a disc, then wrap the dough in plastic wrap. Refrigerate the dough overnight.

Remove the dough from the refrigerator and let come to room temperature for about 30 minutes. Line two sheet pans with parchment paper. Place the dough between two sheets of parchment paper and roll it out to a thickness of ¼ inch (6 mm). If the dough sticks, sprinkle it with a little cocoa powder on both sides. Using a 2-inch (5-cm) round cookie cutter, cut out cookies and place them 1 inch (2.5 cm) apart on the prepared sheet pans; reroll scraps once for more cookies. Transfer the pans to the refrigerator and chill for 30 more minutes.

While the dough chills, preheat the oven to 350°F (175°C).

Bake the cookies one pan at a time until puffed and matte, 10 to 11 minutes. Place the pan on a wire rack and let the cookies cool for about 10 minutes. Using a metal spatula, transfer the cookies to another wire rack and let cool completely before moving them, as they are very delicate.

If using the frosting, with a small offset spatula, frost each cookie then top with sprinkles, if you like.

CHEESES, CHERRIES & CHOCOLATES

The traditional French cheese course is served after dessert, but this board combines both courses by adding chocolates, fresh fruits, and a homemade spicy fruit condiment to an array of cheeses. So simple, so easy, and so luxurious. Choose cheeses that are different in texture and flavor such as mimolette, a hard cheese with a fruity and nutty flavor; soft-textured and creamy Camembert or Brie, with a rich and buttery flavor; and a lovely semi-hard toma, with grassy and tangy notes. This is a good place to showcase any fruit, not only fresh cherries, so use whatever you like and is in season. **Serves 4 to 6**

Provençal Fromage Fort (page 138)
Dark Cherry Mostarda (page 139)

ACCOMPANIMENTS
Sliced or torn pain au levain or baguette

Dried cherry crackers, such as Rustic Bakery Artisan Crisps

A variety of 3 or more cheeses (see above)

Fresh Rainier and/or Bing cherries, or dried cherries

Chocolates, such as shards of dark or milk chocolate or chocolate-covered cherries

Sliced chocolate loaf cake

A chunk of honeycomb

Edible flowers, such as nasturtium flowers and leaves, pansies, violets, or rose petals and buds

TO DRINK
Pinot noir or dessert wine

PUTTING IT TOGETHER
Place the fromage fort on a board with a small bowl of the mostarda and the bread and crackers. Arrange the other cheeses on a separate board along with the fresh or dried cherries, chocolates, loaf cake, and honey-comb. Garnish with the flowers and leaves.

Provençal Fromage Fort

Fromage fort means "strong cheese" and is one of the easiest appetizers you can make because it consists of various white cheeses mixed with butter and a little vermouth. This recipe uses three specific cheeses, but you can simply save cheese ends and bits from your fridge, remove any rinds, and make your own version of this spread to serve on crackers or bread or in sandwiches and/or burgers.

Serves 4

¾ cup (3 ounces/85 g) crumbled Roquefort

¾ cup (3 ounces/85 g) shredded white cheddar or Gruyère

¾ cup (3 ounces/85 g) shredded toma

¼ cup (55 g) cold unsalted butter, preferably European style, grated

1 clove garlic, grated

½ teaspoon herbes de Provence

1 teaspoon crushed pink peppercorns, plus more for garnish (optional)

⅓ cup (75 ml) chilled sweet vermouth

Garlic salt

Edible flowers, fresh herb sprigs, or herbes de Provence, for garnish

In the bowl of a food processor, combine the cheeses, butter, garlic, herbes de Provence, and the 1 teaspoon pink peppercorns, if using. Pulse fifteen times to combine the mixture. With the machine running, stream in the vermouth until smooth and creamy. Season with garlic salt.

If serving right away, spoon into a small serving dish and garnish with pink peppercorns, edible flowers, herb sprigs, or herbes de Provence. To store, refrigerate in a jar with a tight-fitting lid for up to 1 week. Remove from the refrigerator about 15 minutes before serving.

Dark Cherry Mostarda

Mostarda, a spicy, mustardy Italian fruit condiment, is an intense, sweet-sour complement to cheese. This version is a heavenly combination of dark cherries, brown sugar, balsamic vinegar, and quatre épices. Try pairing it with creamy cheeses such as Brie spread on baguette slices or crackers.

Makes 1⅛ cups (270 ml) | Serves 4

1 pound (455 g) fresh Bing cherries, pitted, or thawed frozen sweet cherries with juice

⅓ cup (75 ml) red wine, such as pinot noir

⅓ cup (75 ml) balsamic vinegar

¼ cup (44 g) plus 1 tablespoon light brown sugar

½ teaspoon kosher salt

½ teaspoon Quatre Épices (page 80)

¼ teaspoon crushed pink peppercorns

1 dried bay leaf

1 cinnamon stick

2 tablespoons grainy Dijon mustard

In a small saucepan, combine all the ingredients except the mustard and stir with a wooden spoon. Bring to a boil over medium heat and then reduce the heat to low and simmer, stirring occasionally, until thickened, 1 hour to 1 hour and 15 minutes. Remove from the heat and stir in the Dijon. Let cool to room temperature. Discard the bay leaf and cinnamon stick. Serve immediately, or transfer the mostarda to a jar with a tight-fitting lid and refrigerate for up to 2 weeks.

COOKING TIP
If using frozen cherries, the reduction time might take longer.

THE ENORMOUS COOKIE PLATE

This dessert menu, which can be customized to accommodate any size gathering, consists of cookies, cookies, and cookies, all served on a large, beautiful plate, platter, or board. Mix the homemade biscotti and cherry-almond oat bars with specialties from your local bakery to offer a selection of flavors, shapes, sizes, and textures. You can also use any of the other cookies in this book, such as Chocolate-Cinnamon Shortbread (page 135) or Sesame-Almond Shortbread (page 115). **Serves 6 to 8**

Chocolate Chip Biscotti (page 142)
Cherry-Almond Oat Bars (page 145)

ACCOMPANIMENTS
Assorted cookies from your local bakery or bakeries, such as amaretti,
  French macarons, maple sandwich creams, shortbread, pirouette
  wafer cookies, and chocolate Pocky sticks

TO DRINK
Champagne or espresso

PUTTING IT TOGETHER
Choose a large plate or platter that will fit all or many of your cookies. Arrange the biscotti, cherry-almond oat bars, any other homemade cookies, and any store-bought cookies decoratively on the platter.

MAKE IT BEAUTIFUL I used a vintage silver platter and loaded it up abundantly, so choose your prettiest, most elegant plate or platter for this one. When selecting cookies, go for a variety of colors, textures, and flavors. Look for specialty cookies like colorful French macarons, sugar-studded amaretti, and classic shortbread. I love the wrappers from the amaretti in their gorgeous shades of blue, green and red.

Chocolate Chip Biscotti

One of my duties for my first restaurant job was baking the cookies for the cookie plate on the dessert menu at A16 in San Francisco. Sometimes, there were thumbprint cookies, jam bars, pignoli (pine nut) cookies, and shortbread, but always there were biscotti. Here, the crunchy cookies are studded with mini chocolate chips, and scented with chocolate and cinnamon. Make them in advance so you can chill the dough overnight before baking the next day; the pre-baked logs can also be frozen for up to 2 months.

Makes about 5 dozen biscotti

2¾ cups (345 g) all-purpose flour

3½ teaspoons ground cinnamon

1¾ teaspoons baking powder

¾ teaspoon kosher salt

½ cup (115 g) unsalted butter, preferably European style, at room temperature

1¼ cups (250 g) sugar

2 large room-temperature eggs, lightly beaten

2 teaspoons vanilla extract

1 cup (175 g) mini semisweet chocolate chips

In a large bowl, combine the flour, cinnamon, baking powder, and salt; stir with a whisk to blend. In a stand mixer fitted with a paddle attachment, cream the butter on medium speed until fluffy, about 1 minute. Gradually add the sugar and continue mixing for 2 to 3 minutes. Scrape down the sides of the mixer and the paddle, then add the eggs and vanilla and mix until blended, about 1 more minute. With the mixer on low speed, gradually add the flour mixture ¼ cup (30 g) at a time until just incorporated. Fold in the chocolate chips using a rubber spatula.

On a lightly floured surface, divide the dough into three equal parts. Roll each part into a log 13 inches (33 cm) long. Wrap tightly in plastic wrap and refrigerate overnight or for up to 1 week.

To bake the biscotti, preheat the oven to 350°F (175°C). Line a sheet pan with two layers of parchment paper. Working with one dough log at a time (leave the others in the refrigerator), unwrap and place the log in the center of the prepared pan. Bake until the log is lightly golden and slightly soft to the touch, 20 to 21 minutes. The log will spread and flatten. Transfer the pan to a wire rack and let cool for 20 minutes. Meanwhile, lower the oven temperature to 325°F (165°C).

Transfer the cookie log to a cutting board. Using a sharp serrated knife, gently cut the cookies diagonally into slices that are ¼ inch (6 mm) thick; to slice, cut directly down without sawing.

Transfer the biscotti slices back on the sheet pan, cut side up and spaced slightly apart, and bake for 7 minutes. Using a small offset spatula, carefully turn the slices over and bake for an additional 7 minutes. Let the biscotti cool completely on the sheet pan set on the wire rack. The cookies will crisp as they cool.

To bake the remaining cookies, increase the oven temperature to 350°F (175°C) and repeat as directed, baking one log at a time. Serve now, or store in an airtight container at room temperature for up to 4 days.

Cherry–Almond Oat Bars

Who can resist a cookie made with fruity jam layered between a buttery crust and a crumbly topping? These beautiful bars are made with cherry jam, old-fashioned oats, and toasted almonds. They shine on a cookie plate and are also good for breakfast, snacks, and picnics. Be sure to use slivered almonds, not sliced, and old-fashioned oats, which cook more slowly and give a chewier texture than instant oats. Other jams or preserves can easily be substituted for the cherry jam, such as strawberry, blackberry, or even fig jam.

Makes 18 bars | Serves 6 to 8

½ cup (55 g) slivered almonds

1¼ cups (110 g) old-fashioned oats

1¼ cups (165 g) all-purpose flour

¾ cup (165 g) packed light or dark brown sugar

½ teaspoon baking soda

½ teaspoon ground cinnamon

¼ teaspoon kosher salt

½ cup (115 g) plus 2 tablespoons cold salted butter, preferably European-style, finely diced

¾ cup (180 ml) cherry jam or preserves

Preheat the oven to 350°F (175°C). Butter a 9-inch (23-cm) square baking pan and line it with parchment paper, leaving an overhang on two sides.

Spread the almonds on a small sheet pan and bake, stirring once or twice, until lightly toasted, about 7 minutes. Set aside and let cool. Transfer the cooled almonds to a cutting board and coarsely chop. Set aside 2 tablespoons to top the bars before baking.

In a large bowl, combine the remaining almonds, the oats, flour, sugar, baking soda, cinnamon, and salt. Add the butter and, using your hands, crumble everything together until the butter is in pea-size pieces. Be careful not to overwork.

Press about 2¾ cups (385 g) of the crust mixture into the prepared pan. Transfer the remaining mixture to a small bowl (this will be the topping). Use a small juice glass or jar to press the crust mixture into an even layer in the pan. Refrigerate the crust and freeze the topping mixture for 15 minutes.

Spread the cherry jam over the crust in an even layer, leaving a ¼-inch (6-mm) border on all sides. Sprinkle the topping mixture evenly over the cherry jam, then sprinkle with the reserved 2 tablespoons almonds. Using a large offset spatula, gently press the topping down into the jam. Bake until golden and slightly puffed in the center, 25 to 27 minutes.

Transfer the pan to a wire rack and let the bars cool completely, about 1 hour. To remove the bars from the pan, run a small offset spatula around the edges and, using the parchment overhang, gently lift the bars and place them on a cutting board. Cut the bars into 3-inch (7.5-cm) squares, then cut each square diagonally to yield 18 triangles. Serve immediately, or store in an airtight container at room temperature for up to 4 days.

STRAWBERRY FIELDS FOR EVERYONE

In my opinion, the best time of the year isn't Christmas—it's strawberry season, when this sweet berry is at its peak ripeness and available at the farmers' markets. This board is my love letter to my favorite red fruit. This seasonal menu features individual strawberry galettes—a kind of rustic, free-form tart. They are even better served with scoops of strawberry gelato. The mini strawberry and basil cannoli are really special. I round out the board with fresh strawberries, store-bought (or homemade) strawberry jam cookies, and chocolate bark with freeze-dried strawberries. This is my quintessential birthday dessert menu. **Serves 4 to 6**

Summer Thyme Strawberry Galettes (page 148)
Strawberry–Basil Cannoli (page 151)

ACCOMPANIMENTS
Fresh strawberries
Store-bought strawberry jam cookies
White chocolate–strawberry bark, or any strawberry candy
Strawberry or vanilla gelato, or whipped cream

TO DRINK
Strawberry tea, iced or hot

PUTTING IT TOGETHER
Think pink for this menu! Arrange the galettes on a silver platter—or your favorite pretty platter—along with the fresh strawberries. Arrange the cannoli, cookies, and white chocolate bark on another pretty plate. Add additional fresh strawberries to a cute linen-lined basket or bowl; I used a pink-colored strawberry basket with the prettiest strawberries from the farmers' market. For visual impact, I used brightly-colored bakeware to display some of the galettes. Pre-scoop the gelato, keep them on a small sheet pan in the freezer, and then serve it as requested on the galettes, à la mode style. If using whipped cream, serve in a small bowl.

Summer Thyme Strawberry Galettes

Irresistible mini galettes with a strawberry filling are elegant, beautiful, and intensely strawberry. Fresh thyme adds its special green, herby scent.

Makes 4 mini galettes | Serves 4

Crust

1 cup (125 g) all-purpose flour

3 tablespoons whole-wheat pastry flour

1 teaspoon granulated sugar

Leaves from 2 sprigs thyme

⅛ teaspoon kosher salt

7 tablespoons (100 g) cold unsalted butter, preferably European-style, cut into small cubes and frozen for 5 minutes

4 to 4½ tablespoons (60 to 75 ml) ice-cold vodka or ice water

Filling

8 small fresh strawberries, hulled and thinly sliced

1 tablespoon light brown sugar

½ teaspoon cornstarch

Pinch of kosher salt

Grated zest and juice of ½ lemon

Leaves from 1 fresh thyme sprig, plus more for garnish (optional)

1 large egg whisked with 1 teaspoon water, for egg wash

2 tablespoons turbinado sugar (optional)

Vanilla or strawberry gelato or ice cream, or whipped cream, for serving (optional)

To make the crust, in the bowl of a food processor, pulse the flours, sugar, thyme leaves, and salt together five times. Add the butter and pulse until the butter is the size of peas. Add the vodka 1 tablespoon at a time, pulsing until the dough comes together. Turn the dough out onto a lightly floured surface or pastry board and form into a ball with your hands, then flatten into a disc. Wrap tightly with plastic wrap and refrigerate overnight.

Line a small sheet pan with parchment paper. Remove the dough from the refrigerator and let it stand at room temperature for about 15 minutes. Place the dough between two pieces of parchment paper or on a lightly floured surface and roll out into an 11-inch (28-cm) round. If the dough crumbles, just pinch it back together. Using a 4½-inch (11-cm) round cutter, cut out 4 pastry rounds and place them on the prepared sheet pan used earlier; refrigerate for 20 minutes.

Meanwhile, make the filling. In a small bowl, combine the strawberries, sugar, cornstarch, salt, lemon zest and juice, and leaves from 1 thyme sprig and stir to mix. Let stand while the pastry rounds chill, stirring once or twice.

Working with one pastry round at a time and keeping the rest refrigerated, place 1 heaping tablespoon of strawberries on the dough. Pleat the edges of the dough all around the pastry, press the pleats to seal, and return the pastry to the refrigerator. Repeat with the remaining pastry rounds and filling. Place the galettes in the freezer for at least 1 hour or as long as overnight.

To bake the galettes, line a sheet pan with parchment paper and preheat the oven to 425°F (220°C). Press the pleats down, then brush the galettes with the egg wash and sprinkle with the turbinado sugar, if using. Transfer the galettes to the prepared sheet pan and bake until the filling is bubbling and the pastry is golden brown, 20 to 25 minutes.

Place the sheet pan with the galettes on a wire rack for 10 minutes, then transfer the galettes from the pan to the wire rack. Serve warm or at room temperature, with scoops of gelato, if desired.

Strawberry–Basil Cannoli

These famous Sicilian pastries are made from fried pastry shells filled with sweetened ricotta and studded with candied fruit. My version uses premade mini cannoli shells and includes two of my favorite ingredients: strawberries and basil. Look for the cannoli shells in Italian food specialty stores or online, or make your own!

Makes 12 mini cannoli | Serves 4 to 6

1 cup (245 g) whole-milk ricotta

1 cup (21 g) freeze-dried strawberries

¼ cup (40 g) confectioners' sugar, sifted, plus more for dusting

1 tablespoon finely chopped fresh basil, plus small whole leaves for garnish

Pinch of kosher salt

12 store-bought mini cannoli shells

Sliced fresh strawberries or fresh basil leaves, for garnish

Put the ricotta in a sieve lined with two layers of damp cheesecloth and set over a bowl. Refrigerate for at least 8 hours or up to overnight. Discard any liquid.

Using a mini food processor, process the 1 cup freeze-dried strawberries to a powder. Alternatively, place the strawberries in a zippered plastic bag and pulverize them with a rolling pin. Sift the powdered strawberries through a fine-mesh sieve set over a bowl. Add the ¼ cup (40 g) confectioners' sugar to the strawberry powder and whisk until blended. Add the drained ricotta and gently whisk until combined. Fold in the chopped basil and the salt. Cover and refrigerate for 1 hour.

Fit a pastry bag with a star or round tip and add the ricotta filling to the pastry bag. Pipe all but about 1 tablespoon of the filling inside the cannoli shells. Dust lightly with confectioners' sugar. Pipe a tiny dollop of the remaining filling onto the center of each of the filled shells and top with a slice of fresh strawberry or a basil leaf. Serve right away.

MAKE IT BEAUTIFUL We used micro-basil to dress up the cannoli, but you can also use the small leaves of regular basil. Be sure to use the prettiest leaves that you can find to garnish. You can also sprinkle a bit more of the freeze-dried strawberry powder over the cannoli before serving.

HALVA–LICIOUS BOARD

Halva is a Middle Eastern confection made from tahini and sugar. It comes in many different flavors, such as pistachio, chocolate, and coconut. This dessert board features chewy blondies made with halva, tahini, and pistachios, as well as several kinds of purchased halva and a host of embellishments like dried fruit, nuts, and honeycomb. My favorite halva and tahini brand is Seed + Mill, who have a brick and mortar in New York City's Chelsea Market, and have now expanded to online and specialty markets. This is a delightful dessert menu for a cozy girl's night. **Serves 4 to 6**

Tahini, Halva & Pistachio Blondies (page 155)

ACCOMPANIMENTS

Three types of store-bought halva, such as plain, pistachio, cherry, or chocolate, preferably from Seed + Mill

Chopped pistachios, dried cherries, chocolate chunks, toasted sesame seeds, or other garnishes depending on the flavors of halva

Fresh cherries, sliced apricots, and red currants

Dates

Halva-coated pecans or toasted pecans

A hunk of honeycomb

TO DRINK

Mint tea

PUTTING IT TOGETHER

Add the blondies to a wide, shallow bowl. Choose a large, pretty board and top with the three flavors of halva studded and sprinkled with corresponding garnishes, such as pistachios, dried cherries, and chocolate chunks. Arrange the fresh fruit, dates, pecans, and honeycomb on the board. Include small dessert plates.

MAKE IT BEAUTIFUL Go for abundance, color, and a variety of flavors and textures when styling this sweets board. Choosing seasonal fruit that is readily available to you will always yield the best results. Slice the halva right before serving.

Tahini, Halva & Pistachio Blondies

The first time that I had tahini and halva I was in New York. I had attended a food styling workshop with Susan Spungen and Yossy Arefi and met Rachel Simons, the owner and CEO of Seed + Mill, and our goody bags included tahini and halva. I was hooked! I do love brownies, but I've also never met a blondie I didn't like. This recipe uses tahini, pistachios, halva, and toasted sesame seeds for a gooey blondie with warm Middle Eastern flavors.

Makes 16 mini blondies | Serves 4 to 6

¼ cup (55 g) unsalted butter, preferably European-style

1 cup (220 g) packed light brown sugar

¼ cup (60 ml) tahini, well stirred

2 large eggs, at room temperature

2 teaspoons vanilla extract

1 cup (125 g) all-purpose flour

¾ teaspoon ground cardamom

½ teaspoon kosher salt

½ cup (75 g) unsalted shelled pistachios, toasted and coarsely chopped

½ cup (75 g) plain halva, crumbled

¼ cup (40 g) plus 1 tablespoon white sesame seeds, lightly toasted (see page 28)

Flaky salt, for sprinkling (optional)

Arrange an oven rack in the center of the oven and preheat the oven to 350°F (175°C). Butter an 8-inch (20-cm) square metal pan and line it with parchment paper, leaving an overhang on two sides.

In a small saucepan over low heat, gently melt the butter on low heat (do not brown), then pour it into a large bowl. Whisk in the sugar, tahini, and the eggs one at a time; whisk in the vanilla.

Sift in the flour, cardamom, and salt and stir with a rubber spatula until blended, making sure to scrape down the sides and the bottom of the bowl. The batter will be slightly stiff and the texture of thick peanut butter. Fold in the pistachios, halva, and ¼ cup (40 g) of the sesame seeds, reserving the rest for the top. Transfer the batter to the prepared pan and use an offset spatula to smooth the surface evenly. Top with the remaining 1 tablespoon of sesame seeds and the flaky salt, if using.

Bake until the edges are golden brown and slightly pulled away from the pan and the center is slightly cracked and puffed but still gooey, about 25 minutes (or slightly longer if you want a firmer texture). Let cool completely in the pan on a wire rack, about 30 minutes, before lifting the blondies from the pan using the two sides of the parchment paper.

Cut into 1½-inch (4-cm) squares using a warm knife, and wiping it clean after each cut. Serve immediately, or store in an airtight container at room temperature for up to 4 days.

MAKE IT BEAUTIFUL Wipe the knife clean while cutting each slice to make neat squares. Also, scatter extra toasted sesame seeds over the top, if desired.

INDEX

ACKNOWLEDGMENTS

To Leslie Jonath, my agent: I will never forget when you reached out to me one cold December morning and asked, "Are you interested in thinking about doing a book in 2021? I'd love to brainstorm!" and my reply was "Absolutely yes!" That was the beginning. So, thank you for believing that I could do this and for the faith you had in me; I owe it all to you Leslie.

Thank you to the team at Cameron + Company for trusting me to write this book and style the photographs. You let me share my voice and storytelling through my recipes, and I thank you for all your support and belief in a first-time author.

To Kim Laidlaw, my editor: I am still learning so much from you. From my very first baking classes at the San Francisco Cooking School until now, it is incredible how this has come full circle. I look to you for direction, expertise, and guidance. Thank you for helping me convey my words more succinctly and for working with me in this creative capacity.

To my brilliant photographer, Marie Reginato: When I say that this book is as much yours as mine, I mean it wholeheartedly. Thank you for your countless hours of work, editing, and doing everything to get it 100 percent right.

To Susan Spungen, who I have had the pleasure of meeting and being one of your students more than once, I extend my deepest gratitude. I continue to learn from you and am inspired by your incredible body of work daily. Thank you for all of your advice and for helping steer me on this project, and for writing a brilliant foreword.

Molly DeCoudreaux who opened the door and hired me for my very first food styling gig for *Feed Your People* and introduced me to Leslie Jonath and the world of food photography.

To my assistant Emily Cooper: From the very first moment that I met you, I knew that I wanted to have you involved in the making of this book. Thank you to you for all of your testing, Trader Joe's runs in the morning, and cheerful support. Having you on set made it all the more special! Mostly, thank you for being you and always being such a positive and delightful friend.

To my assistant Lauren Ruben: Thank you for always having my back! I love what brought us together are in fact cookbooks, community, and cooking. Thank you for your willingness to join us in the early days on set and for providing a calmness, serenity, and beauty. Thank you for your grocery store runs, ordering lunches, and visits with Nala—we love you!

To Shelley Lindgren, thank you so much for taking a chance on a very green pastry chef at your restaurant, A16. You have paved the way to my culinary career. Who knew that helping you select makeup at Saks Fifth Avenue at NARS for the James Beard Awards would open so many doors? You are and have always been an inspiration to me and for that, I am truly grateful.

To Kate Leahy: Thank you for giving my proposal a read in the very beginning and for helping me navigate my story. Thank you for your support, kindness, and all your advice over the writing phase of this cookbook. Also, that almond tip works like a dream every time!

To David, my husband and production manager: How can I say thank you? I cannot imagine doing this without you! You were the one who said to me, "Are you making one of those nibble board things with a few kinds of cheeses?" And I knew I had to embrace this eating style for the rest of my life. Thank you for helping teach me to stop and smell the roses and for being my favorite recipe taster. You are my very best friend, lover, and soul mate. It has been a joy making you snacks to test, (some actually were quite inedible), sending samples to your workmates, and packing lunch with oodles of recipes waiting to be discovered in the pages of this book. Thank you for being my favorite stage hand and hand model. I love you to the moon and back.

CAMERON + COMPANY
149 Kentucky Street, Suite 7
Petaluma, CA 94952
www.cameronbooks.com

CREATIVE DIRECTOR Iain R. Morris
MANAGING EDITOR Jan Hughes
EDITORIAL ASSISTANT Krista Keplinger

EXECUTIVE EDITOR Kim Laidlaw
DESIGNER Emily Studer
FOOD STYLING ASSISTANTS Emily Cooper & Lauren Ruben
COPY EDITOR Carolyn Miller
PROOFREADER Amy Treadwell
INDEXER Ken Della Penta

Library of Congress Control Number: 2023952393
ISBN: 978-1-949480-51-1

10 9 8 7 6 5 4 3 2 1

Printed and bound in China

~≪≪≪~

CONTRIBUTORS

Bebe Black Carminito is a food stylist, recipe developer, content
creator, and professional makeup artist. She co-runs and oversees
three global cookbook clubs. Her foray into cookbooks was *The
California Date Cookbook* as well as styling for *52 Shabbats*.
Bebe attended the San Francisco Cooking School and started her
culinary career at A16, an acclaimed restaurant in San Francisco.
She resides in San Francisco in her teeny-tiny apartment with her
husband and best friend, David Carminito.

Susan Spungen, is a cook, food stylist, recipe developer, and
author. She was the founding food editor and editorial director for
food at Martha Stewart Living Omnimedia from its inception in
1991 until 2003. She was the culinary consultant and food stylist
on the feature films *Julie & Julia*, *It's Complicated*, and *Eat, Pray,
Love*. She is the author of *Open Kitchen: Inspired Food for Casual
Gatherings*, *Recipes: A Collection for the Modern Cook*, *What's
a Hostess to Do?*, and *Strawberries (A Short Stack Edition)*, and
most recently, *Veg Forward: Super-Delicious Recipes that Put
Produce at the Center of Your Plate*. She is also the author of
Susanality, a popular Substack newsletter. She lives in New York
City and East Hampton, NY.

Marie Reginato is a photographer, cooking video host, and author
of *Alternative Vegan* and *The Ultimate Vegan Cookbook*. She lives
in Los Angeles, California.

Thank you to the brands who have graciously donated product for
the recipe developing, testing and photography phases: Anne's Toum,
Brooklyn Delhi, Coro Foods, Exau Olive Oil, Flour + Water Pasta, Graze +
Gather Co., Great Jones, Guildford Green, Oaktown Spice, Rustic Bakery,
Seed + Mill, SOS Bakeshop, That's My Jam, and Viski Craft.

Thank you to the members of my amazing Instagram cookbook-club
community: #getcookingcookbookclub, #proofcollectivecookbookclub,
and #qbcookbookclub. I could not have written this book without you!
Danaen Balisteri, Mary Borowiec, Saira Campbell, Karen Carbone,
Sylvie Charles, Sherry Constable, Emily Cooper, Gretchen Dalrymple,
Angela DeCenzo, Maddie DeWitt, Christina Di Feo Petrella, Dana Eastland,
Lizzy Elliot, Zoe Friesen, Anagha Godbole, Lisa Goldstein, Carly Hackbarth,
Jan Hammock, Chandler Henry, Priya Kane, Clare Langan, Camille Laws,
Kate Leahy, Monique Llamas, Suzette Lopez, Sandra Maltry, Kristi Mundt,
Petra Orlowski, Maia Paul, Alexa Prendergast, Shahla Rashid, Katie
Rodriguez, Diane Russell, Pam Schwartz, Micah Siva, Anne Sjostrom
Reynolds, Luke Smedley, Sarah Ubertaccio, Mayumi Wardrop,
Steph Whitten, Kayla Zola

RECIPE CONTRIBUTORS

To all of my recipe contributors, I could not have done this without you.
Thank you for entrusting your recipes and your family recipes to me
for this cookbook. When I first set out to think about the concept for this
book, one of the most important things to me was to collaborate with
like-minded food creatives while embracing your food cultures. I wanted
to give a voice to your recipes and to your vision.

Anna Voloshyna is a Ukrainian American chef, food blogger, and author
of the acclaimed cookbook *BUDMO! Recipes from a Ukrainian Kitchen*.
Born and raised in Ukraine, Anna's expertise in this cuisine has earned
her numerous accolades, including features in the *New York Times*,
Food & Wine, and other publications. @voloshynacooks

Amisha Gurbani is a recipe developer, photographer, food blogger, and the
creator of the Jam Lab website, where she shares vegetarian recipes and
desserts inspired by her Indian upbringing. She is the author of *Mumbai
Modern* and writes for the *San Francisco Chronicle*. @thejamlab

Christine Gallary is a Chinese American food editor at *The Kitchn* and a
recipe developer. Her favorite cuisine is Cantonese, but French food is a
close second, as she graduated from Le Cordon Bleu in Paris. @cgallary

Eric Lundy is a food stylist, recipe developer, private chef, and cooking
instructor. A consummate Francophile, his knowledge and love of French
food inform his styling, consulting, and teaching. @ericlundyfood

Micah Siva is a chef, cookbook author, registered dietitian, recipe
writer, and food photographer specializing in modern Jewish cuisine.
Micah shares Jewish-inspired, plant-forward recipes on her blog,
Nosh with Micah. @noshwithmicah

Rezel Kealoha is a food photographer, food stylist, writer, and Filipino
food advocate. She shares recipes on her eponymous blog, which
focuses on Filipino ingredients and flavors. @rezelkealoha

Steve Drapeau and Katia Berberi are the husband-and-wife founders
of Anne's Toum, an authentic Lebanese garlic sauce. They envisioned
sharing Katia's family's toum recipe with the masses and have enjoyed
sharing this garlicky goodness with people since 2020. @annestoum

"Bye-bye boring boards! Just when you think you've seen one too many charcuterie boards, Bebe swoops in with innovative ways to share snacks all day long. Not only are the recipes stellar, but the boards themselves are just gorgeous. Call your friends—it's time for a party!"

—JODI LIANO, *founder of the San Francisco Cooking School and cookbook author*

"*The Curated Board* is how we all love to eat and entertain. The detailed themes for the boards could be used for a multitude of occasions year-round and even get you packed up to enjoy nature in style. The menagerie of ingredients makes such a difference and creates fun flavors while trying different combinations. You'll want to try them all. Beverage-pairing suggestions were incredibly thoughtful and spot-on. Brava, Bebe!"

—SHELLEY LINDGREN, *James Beard Award–winning sommelier, cookbook author, and restaurateur*

"*The Curated Board* is the cookbook I didn't even know I was craving (both literally and figuratively). From a Lebanese Sheet Pan Brunch to a Picnic in the Park to a Strawberry Fields for Everyone dessert board (and by 'everyone,' Bebe means me—but don't worry, I'll share), this beautifully photographed and styled book has something for all the peeps in your life, from morning to night and every time in between."

—JESSIE SHEEHAN, *author of* Snackable Bakes